WWMD
What Would Mohammed Do?

By

Bob McLeod

© 2002 by Bob McLeod. All rights reserved.

No part of this book may be reproduced, stored in a retrieval system, or transmitted by any means, electronic, mechanical, photocopying, recording, or otherwise, without written permission from the author.

ISBN: 1-4033-2907-9 (e-book)
ISBN: 1-4033-2908-7 (Paperback)

This book is printed on acid free paper.

1stBooks - rev. 03/05/03

Table of Contents

I. **Islam, a Mirror of the Bible Belt**
   1. From Calhoun County to Constantinople 3
   2. The Hagia Sophia Hood 12
   3. Which Allah? 15
   4. Mad About Mohammed 20
   5. Mean Religious People 31
   6. Mother Nature Kills Muslims and Christians 42

II. **The Five Pillars**
   1. Introduction 59
   2. Shahada, *a simple statement* 62
   3. Salat, *praying* 68
   4. Zakat, *giving* 72
   5. The Fast, *self denial* 78
   6. The Hajj, *the crowd gathers* 84

III. **Freedom**
   1. According to the Book 89
   2. Satan, the Adversary is Necessary 102
   3. Birth Pangs 115
   4. Self-Paralysis 126
   5. The Teddy Bear 140
   6. Pathway to Intimacy 146
   7. The Well 159

IV. **Epilogue** 167

WWMD What Would Mohammed Do?

Islam, a Mirror of the Bible Belt

Bob McLeod

From Calhoun County to Constantinople

Jesus' brother James tells us in the Holy Bible *(James 1:25)* that the perfect law of liberty is a mirror. Just what kind of mirror is it? It's a vivid and accurate reflection of one's heart. It's also the Sovereign Creator's requirement of right standing with Him, the prerequisite for entering His perfect Kingdom.

When we look into this mirror, we not only see ourselves in the light of His perfect law and how unacceptable and imperfect we are, but, as we keep looking, we will also begin to see His provision for making us acceptable. That's why James called it the law of liberty rather than the law of bondage.

Looking into the perfect law of liberty causes us to look beyond what we pretend to be and behold who we really are. Now, that can be frightening, but liberty means freedom and, if we truly want to be free, we must be honest enough to look, to keep looking, and respond to what is revealed.

There are two things we instinctively do to avoid the pain and personal condemnation of looking into the Law of Liberty. One is to shift the blame. The other is to make excuses. If we're doing either, then we're not being honest with ourselves and with our Maker, and no progress can be made!

If I become offended, shift the blame, find fault, and point a self-righteous finger at anyone else, then it's impossible for me to see my own heart. Therefore, I'm doomed to remain in the personal, lonely torment of self-justification, all the while blaming others.

The "Bible Belt" is a slang term used for a geographical region in the South and midsection of the United States—areas that host large groups of fundamentalist Christians. Religion has always been an important part of American life. Since the 1600's over eighty-five percent of the population has participated in some kind of church activity. Towards the end of the Seventeenth Century, however, religious fervor took on an even greater ferocity. It was then that America experienced its first great revival and today's fundamentalist Bible belt is a direct result.

The "Great Awakening", which swept the British Isles, infiltrated the American Colonies. The Southern states, especially, received this "new birth" with fervor. Some said it was a result of the great population of Blacks below the Mason-Dixon Line. Others said it was because the Southerner thought he was closer to God than anyone else. It simply depended on who was doing the talking.

In recent years the exponential increase in technology has made us all much closer neighbors. This has caused the religious influences of the Bible belt and the rest of the country to integrate; therefore, the Bible belt and American Christianity have in some respects, become synonymous terms.

I was born in the Bible belt. My Granddad and Dad were both Baptist Preachers and I've been called one too. But the coat and tie didn't fit. I'm really just a country boy poet and songwriter in blue jeans and T-shirt with a guitar.

It took a number of years and numerous heartbreaks, but looking away from what I thought were the expectations and judgments of other people and looking instead into the perfect law of liberty has helped me begin to discover who I was born to be. I believe that happens to anyone who will dare to look.

When I was thirty years old I was chemically dependent, miserable and severely depressed. I had been for a number of years. I expressed my torment through the songs I was writing.

Each time I saw the undertaker bury the cold, clammy, waxed remains of a friend or member of my family, I became more critical, cynical, and sacrilegious. I was drowning in a sea of self-pity and shame, fighting the guilt by shifting the blame.

"If God is love, then why do people suffer and die? If there is a God then I don't like Him!" was my rapid response to any Christian who approached me, trying to get me saved.

It was 1978, 3 AM one morning. I thought I was alone. Kneeling at the foot of my bed, I cried out to the Lord Jesus Christ, and for the first time, I realized that I wasn't alone at all. He was with me and had been with me all along. I began to receive the love of God that morning. Jesus became my best Friend, and my love for Him continues to grow with each passing day.

Why did I cry out to Jesus? Being raised in the Bible belt, I'd obviously heard a lot about Him. That's probably the reason. Had I been born a Turk and raised in a Muslim community, I probably would have cried out to Allah. But I wasn't, and I didn't. I cried out to Jesus and a miraculous, dramatic change began taking place within me.

One of the immediate, noticeable changes that took place was in the songs I was writing. I went from crying and singing the blues to crying and singing praises. Tears of sorrow became tears of joy!

Psalm 40:2,3
"He also brought me up out of the miry clay and set my feet upon a rock, and established my steps. He has put a new song in my mouth—a song of praise to our God..."

Hope was birthed in my heart and I began to have a burning passion to share that hope with others, particularly those who were in the same nightmare I had been in.

For the first several years I played it safe and stayed close to home. I became more and more involved in our small community Baptist Church. This was a season of becoming more intimately acquainted with the Lord Jesus and His Word. Then, very gradually, He started using the songs to open doors into some unusual, interesting, sometimes even hostile and dangerous places.

Since 1985, I've been privileged to go and befriend people from all walks of life in a variety of subcultures. Everywhere I've been, I've met those who are hurting, confused, broken, grieved, and struggling. Many have lost all hope.

I've met them on death row, in hospices, nursing homes, jails, mental institutions, juvenile detention centers, half way houses, back streets, bars, dope houses, punk rock festivals, and even highbrow, exclusive English boarding schools.

The most fascinating and unusual places to me, however, have been churches. I've been invited to share in Christian churches of almost every imaginable persuasion on Saturday and Sunday, circus and cemetery. What incredible diversities we have!

From "Gates of Hell Won't Prevail:"

> *"Every street corner's got a church.*
> *Every church sings a different tune.*
> *Some say Jesus just arrived. Others say He's coming soon.*
> *Some will drag you in. Some will kick you out.*
> *Seems self-righteous and absurd.*
> *So many disagree, yet all claim authority*
> *In God's Holy Word."*

During autumn of 1999, I took part in a concert tour throughout the United Kingdom with a youth choir from South Africa. After one of the concerts, a lady who is a Missionary in Turkey approached me.

"The type of music you do is becoming quite popular in Istanbul," she said. "Would you be interested in coming over?"

Before I thought, I said, "Sure! Where's Istanbul? Is that anywhere near Constantinople?" Then I remembered an old Broadway Tune. "Istanbul is Constantinople."

I began to seriously pray, trying to listen to the Lord to determine if indeed it was His will that I go. I'm by nature a homebody and I certainly didn't want to show up in a country on the other side of the planet that was ninety-nine percent Muslim. That is, if God were not leading me there!

All I'd ever heard about Muslims was bad! I had recently heard about Mike Tyson becoming a Muslim and then biting off Evander Holyfield's (a Christian's) ear!

"Are them Turkey Muslims militant?" I wondered. "Would a guitar pickin', country boy, with a southern drawl, preaching Jesus, be thrown into a prison with both his hands cut off? Would I ever see my family again?"

After several more email exchanges, God confirmed that it was His will for me to go, and my dear friend, Tim Skinner, was to go with me. What happened to us there was totally unexpected. Though we found ourselves in a drastically different culture, we felt strangely at home.

People are people. We may speak a different language. We may eat and dress differently. We may have a different way of looking at life, yet we are all basically the same and have the same basic instincts and needs.

We have our villains and we have our heroes. We flee rejection and we gravitate toward acceptance. We are typically fearful, insecure and suspicious of strangers or other people who aren't "like us."

All of us grieve and cry as loved ones die. We continually live under a mysterious cloud of the death angel that is coming to take each of us away, often without notice. Though we may not like it, and though we may try to ignore it, planet earth remains death row: hence, the birth of religion.

The superstitious ways we deal with the haunting reality of suffering and dying is diverse. We are lost and frightened creatures desperately fighting to find a thread of hope. But most of the time, we're hiding under a cloud of pretense or else "throwing in the towel," that is, giving up entirely, "burying our head in the sand," and trying not to think about it.

There comes an incredible wonder and joy when we stop feeling threatened by people who have a different worldview than we've been trained to have. If we'll be willing, as much as possible, to put aside our indoctrination and prejudices, to be open, teachable and accepting of anyone and everyone— then we'll discover a faith that is real and we will certainly endure every storm of life. We will also find the key that will free us from the fear of death.

It really doesn't matter if we have squinted eyes, moles on our foreheads, or wear a turban or a veil. We may have the familiar stench of body odor or the store bought fragrance of Dial soap and Ban Roll-On. We may be ghostly white, charcoal black or anything in-between. People belong to God, and all people are beautiful, worth noticing and worthy of affection and attention.

Even though others might be different from us, they are still due dignity and respect. God is pro-choice. He gives each one a choice to make. Therefore, even though our opinions may not be sacred, our God-given ability to have them is. And just because others see from a different perspective than I do, doesn't mean that I have a right to judge them as wrong!

This book is about the incredible similarities between many professing Christians in America and the Bible Belt, and our neighbors in another part of the world who claim Allah is God and Mohammed his prophet and messenger.

There is a growing war between the two while both are basically saying the same thing. Muslim extremists take verses of the Bible out of context, and condemn the Christians, while Christian extremists take verses of the Quran out of context and assault the Muslims.

It's certainly not in my heart to demean people of either faith. My desire is to simply share God's love and thereby expose the bondage and torment of self-justification and "do it yourself salvation."

May we not "point the finger" and dwell on what we perceive to be wrong but rather, let us rejoice in what we're beginning to recognize as being right! The glorious Truth will indeed set one free, and we can be free indeed!

From "We'd Rather Lift Jesus Up:"

> "Why get all wrapped up in hell when Heaven's comin' down?
> We'd rather lift Jesus up instead of puttin' each other down!"

WWMD What Would Mohammed Do?

As we come in humility and honesty, and gaze into the mirror and see the striking similarities of these two cultures of religious people, we will begin to see ourselves more clearly. The process may seem awkward and even somewhat painful at first, but the end result will certainly be life changing and well worth it.

Tim and I made it back home to our friends and family in the familiar surroundings of the Bible belt. We've still got both of our hands but our hearts will never be the same. I'm privileged to share here what we've been learning with you.

If, while reading this, you find yourself becoming offended, perhaps you're getting too close to the mirror and don't like what you see. If this is the case, I urge you, please consider why you're offended, forgive the writer and read on. You'll be glad you did. Offered in the love of our Lord and Savior, Jesus Christ.

Bob McLeod,
Osh Gosh, Alabama
April 2002

Bob McLeod

The Hagia Sophia Hood

Tim and I were guests at a hotel located on the Historic Peninsula of Istanbul, one block from the historic Sultan Ahmet Mosque often referred to as the *"Blue Mosque."* The hotel is also about two blocks from the Hagia Sophia, a Roman monument constructed in the Byzantine Age.

The Sultan Ahmet Mosque was constructed by the fourteenth Ottoman Sultan who ruled AD 1603-1607. It is the greatest and most splendid mosque of Istanbul. There is a huge fountain for ablutions *(Bible Belt folks call 'um baptizins')* in the middle of the courtyard. It has six corners and six columns, thirty domes on twenty-six granite columns. The Mosque is known all over the world as the *"Blue Mosque'* because of the tiles and embellishments, which are mostly in blue with green colors on the walls and the domes.

The Mosque emanates an ominous and hypnotic presence. The six minarets that surround the domes give it the eerie appearance of a huge spacecraft visiting from another galaxy.

One would have to see it to believe it, particularly at night. It stands there glowing and reflecting a countless number of colored lights, sending forth the strange and mystical aura that she's about to come alive and, indeed she does!

Five times a day she sings brazenly loud, with an audacious authority, refusing to be ignored. Her huge loudspeakers intrude upon the day's activities as she blasts the Aramaic call to prayer. Her anthem is echoed by a number of other mosques' loud speakers in the distance. Believe me, it could give a couple of Alabama country boys the creeps! It sounded to us like Ray Stephens' impersonation of Ahab the Arab, but we definitely kept that to ourselves!

Across the street from the Blue Mosque there's a beautifully manicured park leading to the other imposing structure named the Hagia Sophia. Hagia Sophia is an adjective referring to the God in Christianity. It means *"divine wisdom."* The building was constructed in AD 537 and was a Christian Church for 916 years. After Istanbul was conquered, it served the Moslems as a mosque for 481 years. Today, it is an amazing and incredible museum housing ancient Christian and Muslim murals and artifacts.

But the most amazing thing to us was that Tim Skinner and Bob McLeod, a couple of *"country bumpkins"* from the back hills of Alabama, were welcomed into this neighborhood. And we weren't there as passing tourists. It was far more intimate than that. In a short period of time we became family.

We met a young man named Hakan the day we arrived. He worked at the hotel and was handsome, incredibly charming, sincere and hospitable. His English wasn't proficient at all, but it was much better than our Turkish. We bought a little inexpensive, paperback English to Turkish translation book and we were constantly thumbing through its pages as we attempted to communicate with

Hakan. Our lengthy conversations were awkward and hilarious. We were all three in a makeshift language course, and our communication skills became only slightly more proficient as time went on.

Hakan insisted on becoming our after hours tour guide. We became very good friends in a short period of time. There were many late-night discussions about his culture and religion. He was born and reared in a devout Muslim home in very much the same way Tim and I were born and raised in Christian homes. What an unlikely group we were!

To our surprise Hakan would weep as he talked of his love for Jesus. *"I know Jesus."* He said. *"But you Christians say that He died on a cross. That's not true. Allah would never have allowed His prophet to be mistreated and die that way!"*

WWMD What Would Mohammed Do?

Which Allah?

Many Muslims believe that Christians worship three gods: the Father, the Son and Mother Mary. And though they consider a three-in-one God to be a gross blasphemy, there remains a deep admiration for Jesus. They adamantly deny that Jesus was God, but do esteem Him as being one of Allah's prophets.

Any Christian would certainly agree that their God is "the One Who is adored, the One Who created all that exists, who has priority over all creation, who is lofty and hidden, who confounds all human understanding." *This is what the Arabic word, Allah actually means.* It is exactly the same word as, in Hebrew, the Jews use for God (Eloh), *the same word Jesus Christ used in Aramaic when He prayed to God.* God has an identical name in Judaism, Christianity and Islam.

The truth, however, is not necessarily in a name. The name is but a label, sometimes reflecting the true character, but other times it can be a mask for an imposter.

I know of two men, both named Billy. One minister's life, the other ministered death: *Billy Graham and Billy the Kid.* Their character and worthiness has nothing to do with their name. *Therefore, we mustn't get offended or draw conclusions, arguing over a name.* We must look deeper than that.

The Holy Quran is to Muslims what the Bible is to Christians and Jews. It is sacred scripture. For Muslims, the

Quran is a transcript of God's words, uttered by his messenger, Mohammed the prophet.

Mohammed received the message of Islam when he was forty years of age. According to Muslims, Mohammed is the very last prophet of God. His message, they claim, is a message to all of mankind, especially Jews and Christians. He allegedly was sent to the Jews and Christians to inform them about the true mission of Abraham, Isaac, Jacob, Moses, David and Jesus.

Mohammed is considered by Muslims to be the culmination of all the prophets and messengers that came before him. They claim He purified the previous messages from adulteration and completed the message of God for all of humanity.

Islam accepts the Torah (five books of Moses); other books of Old Testament Prophecy; some of the Psalms of David; and the teachings of Jesus. However, they claim that Jews and Christians have subverted these books and that only the Quran remains infallible. The Quran, Muslims claim is not a replacement of the Jewish and Christian Bible but rather, according to the Quran itself, a confirmation and further revelation.

From the Quran (10:37 AYA / 38 MP)
"This Quran is not such as can be produced by other than Allah; on the contrary it is a confirmation of (revelations) that went before it, and a fuller explanation of the Book." (The Bible).

In the Quran there are many references to the Jewish and Christian Holy Books. In fact, the Quran addresses Christians and Jews as "People of the Book:"

From the Quran:
"O ye people of the Book! Believe in what we have now revealed, confirming what was already with you." (4:47 AYA)

Let's begin our honest search for the real "Allah." I believe that if we'll be open and dare to put aside our prejudices, *the imposter will be made obvious.*

From the Book:
Psalm 119:165
"Great peace have they that love your law and nothing shall offend them."

Hostility, hatred, offense, frustration, finger pointing and self-righteousness are not expressions of the true God. They are obvious expressions of insecurity.

The Spirit of our Creator never reacts. Why should He? He's not insecure. He's almighty God and He's in control! He either waits patiently, or else He responds in love. Often times our Creator's response of love may seem severe, but love is always leading us to the more excellent way and always intends our very best.

According to *Galatians 5:22,23 in the Bible,* people who are led by God's Spirit are *gentle and joyful and their lives are becoming more and more characterized by meekness, temperance, faith and love.*

Often times the truth is hidden behind what we hear being said. I can tell you that I'm a Christian and love the Lord, or I can tell you that I'm a Muslim and adore Allah. But if I were able and willing to be completely honest, I might say instead, "I consider myself a good person because I belong to a religious club of like-minded people. My self-worth is based upon my conforming to the expectations of other club member's—expectations that have been formed by traditions handed down by previous generations. *Therefore, my culture dictates who I think I am.*"

"Sir, what do you believe?" the Baptist deacon was asked. "Why, I believe what my church believes," was his reply.

"Well then, what do you and your church believe?"

The deacon thought a minute and replied, "We believe the same thing."

One of the certain indications that I'm in a religious club, Christian or Muslim, is the way I react if my faith is challenged. If I become angry or offended, then, obviously, I'm insecure and if I'm insecure, then my belief system is based on a false security.

I may never admit it, but my reaction reveals that, deep within me, I'm really not convinced that what I profess to believe is true.

This insecurity causes me to be very closed-minded and intolerant of others. I feel very threatened, defensive and withdrawn around people who aren't in my religious club. I feel like I must avoid people who aren't a part of our club.

WWMD What Would Mohammed Do?

As a matter of fact, if my insecurity is pushed far enough, I may even kill you over what I claim to believe! This is what has been happening in Northern Ireland in past years, all in the name of Christ. This is the same insecurity that has driven the extreme religious terrorists throughout history, including Pope Urban II and Osama Bin Laden.

Bob McLeod

Mad About Mohammed

Human beings, like sheep, are fearful and suspicious by nature. This causes us to connect and huddle with like kind. We tend to find safety and security in our group and are typically afraid to be isolated and alone. Anyone who doesn't conform to our group we perceive to be a threat. *That's how peers can pressure.*

Often times we are so indoctrinated by our culture that we lose any sense of objectivity, and, sometimes all sense of reason. That's why we do some of the most absurd things calling them sane; and at the same time, reject some of the most sensible things, calling them insane!

Welcome to the Human Race

The newborn sure is crying.
Just been slapped on the rear,
Turned upside down, then back around,
Wondering how he ever got here!
Planet earth is your new home.
Little baby, now don't you fret.
If you think this place is weird,
Well, you ain't seen nothin' yet!

Welcome to the Human race, my friend,
Welcome to the Human race.

This is where all the fun begins.
See if you can find your place.
Gonna be pain and rain, fun, and some say,
"Get inner peace from outer space."
Welcome to the Human Race, my friend,
Welcome to the Human Race.
Folks down here stick holes in their ears,
Breathe burning leaves and race like rats.
Bake their head in an oven.
The beauty parlor's where they do that.
Sing about Amazing Grace and how they've been made right,
Next thing you know, the First Church of Love
Has broken out in a fight!
Uh Oh!

In some cultures being big is beautiful. In others, being skinny is. In some cultures it's popular to have plates in your lips; in others, it's bones in your nose and rings around your neck. In some cultures they even stick ornaments in their tongue! *Can you believe that?* Next thing you know, they'll be piercing their nipples and navels! *Surely not!*

There just has to be executives on Madison Avenue and other marketing centers, getting rich, laughing their heads off, wagering on who can make the biggest fools of us! *Remember the "pet rocks?"*

Bob McLeod

Imagine a few years ago two brilliant entrepreneurs having dinner in an expensive New York Restaurant. The conversation might have gone something like this:

"Fred, I'll bet you a million dollars that in five years I can assemble millions of people of all ages and all walks of life, including celebrities, dignitaries and the sophisticated, "high collar" crowd. I'll sell them war paint, rubber tomahawks, and all kinds of make-believe Indian paraphernalia. I can even have them publicly making Indian war cries as they chop the air with their hands and dance in a circle. I'll even have it broadcast on national TV!"

Fred says, "No way Joe! They're not that naïve and gullible! I'll take that bet!"

In five years Fred has to pay as they watch an Atlanta Braves game!

What about the seemingly strange religious things we do? If you're not a Mormon, Joseph Smith's claims seem totally ridiculous. Tracing genealogy and getting baptized for dead people is just too weird for someone who isn't a part of it. And do you really believe that anyone who isn't in the "Christian club" will one day soon be *"left behind?"*

If you're a Bible-Belt Christian raised Southern Baptist, Church of Christ, Pentecostal, or Church of Nazarene, etc., then Islam appears strange, weird and threatening. If you were raised in a Muslim country, what is called Christianity may seem strange, weird and threatening to you.

Let's try to put aside our fears and prejudices and become acquainted with this mystic and very gifted man named Mohammed. Millions of people consider him to be the greatest mind among all the sons of Arabia. When he appeared, Arabia was a desert—a nothing. Out of nothing a New World was fashioned by the spirit of this one man: a new life, a new culture, a new civilization, a new kingdom extended from Morocco to the Indies and influenced the thought and life of three continents: Asia, Africa and Europe.

Let's not prematurely judge Mohammed and his claims without hearing them. As much as is possible, let's lay aside the indoctrination of our culture and see what we can learn from this charismatic leader and those who claim to follow him.

It's recorded that Mohammed was born in the desert of Arabia on April 20, 571. His father, Abdullah, died a few weeks before his birth. His mother died when he was six years old. After his mother's death he went to live with his paternal grandfather. When he was eight his grandfather died and his uncle took him in and raised him.

Little Mohammed grew and became popularly know as 'al-Ameen', which means, "honest, reliable and trustworthy." He was a descendant of Abraham through the lineage of Ishmael and his second son, Kedar.

Mohammed was raised illiterate, unable to read or write, and remained so until his death. As he grew up, he became known for his truthfulness, generosity and sincerity; so much so that he was sought after for his ability to arbitrate in disputes. Historians describe him as calm, meditative and very religious. This is the Muslim's account of Mohammed being revealed as the Prophet:

When he was forty, he took one of his many retreats to Mount Hira for meditation. It was during the month that is now recognized as Ramadan, which is the ninth month of the Islamic calendar when a daily fast is enjoined from dawn until sunset. While Mohammed was there he received the first revelation from the Archangel Gabriel.

On his first appearance Gabriel said to Mohammed, "Iqraa," meaning "read or recite." Mohammed replied, "I cannot read," as he had not received any formal education and did not know how to read or write. The Angel Gabriel then embraced him until he reached the limit of his endurance and after releasing him said again, "Iqraa!" Mohammed's answer was the same as before. Gabriel repeated the embrace for a third time and then asked Mohammed to repeat after him and said:

"Recite in the Name of the Lord Who created! He created man from that which clings. Recite; and thy Lord is most Bountiful, He who has taught by the pen taught man what he knew not."

The revelations he received that day are the first five verses of Surah (meaning chapter) 96 of *the Quran*. This was in the year AD 610.

Mohammed was terrified by the experience and fled the cave of Mt. Hira. *(Quran 81:19-20.)* When he reached his home, tired and frightened, he said to his wife, "Cover me, cover me in a blanket!" After his awe and fear had somewhat subsided, his wife Khadijah asked him why he was so shaken. After he explained, she reassured him by saying, "Allah (the One True God) will not let you down because you are kind to relatives, and you speak only the truth. You help the poor, the orphan and the needy, and you are an honest man.

Khadijah then consulted with her cousin, Waraqa, an old, saintly man, possessing knowledge of previous revelations and scriptures. Waraqa confirmed to her that the visitor was none other than the angel Gabriel who had come to Moses. *He then added that Mohammed was the expected prophet.*

Khadijah accepted the revelation given to her husband as truth and became the first person to accept Islam. She supported her husband in every hardship, and there were many. Khadijah died at the age of sixty-five in the month of Ramadan.

Gabriel reportedly visited the Prophet as commanded by Allah, revealing Ayat (meaning signs, loosely referred to as verses) in Arabic, over a period of twenty-three years. The revelations that he received were sometimes a few verses, a part of a chapter or the whole chapter. Some revelations came down in response to inquiries of nonbelievers.

The revealed verses were recorded on a variety of available materials (leather, palm leaves, bark, shoulder bones of animals), memorized as soon as they were revealed, and were recited in daily prayers by Muslims *(Quran 80:13-16)*. Angel Gabriel taught the order and arrangement of the verses, and the Prophet instructed his several scribes to record verses in that order *(Quran 75:16-19 and 41:42)*

Once a year, the Prophet would recite back to the Angel Gabriel all the verses revealed to him up until that time. This was to authenticate the accuracy of recitation and the order of verses *(Quran 175:106)*. All verses were compiled in the book known as the *Quran.*

The Quran, according to Muslims, does not even contain a word from the Prophet. The *Quran* speaks in the first person, i.e., Allah's commandments to His creation.

The Angel Gabriel also allegedly visited the Prophet throughout his mission, informing and teaching him of events and strategy, as needed to help in the completion of the prophetic mission. The prophet's sayings, actions, and approvals are recorded separately in collections known as Hadith or Sunni, which is considered by Muslims to be another holy book.

The mission of the Prophet Mohammed was to restore the worship of the One True God, the Creator and Sustainer of the universe, as taught by the Prophet Abraham and all the Prophets of God. It was also to demonstrate and complete the laws of moral, ethical, legal, and social conduct and all other matters of significance for humanity at large.

The Quran states that *"Jesus, son of Mary said... "I am indeed the Messenger of God to you, confirming the Torah that is before me and giving good tidings of a messenger who shall come after me whose name shall be Ahmad (Mohammed)." (Sura 61:6)*

Muslims also claim that there are even prophecies in the Christian Bible that point to Mohammed. Among those are:

John 14:16 "I will pray the Father, and He will give you another helper (parakletos, meaning counselor or comforter) to be with you forever." Muslims believe the helper He's referring to in this verse is none other than Mohammed.

Any passage in the Bible that refers to a messenger or prophet to come, Muslims interpret to mean, Mohammed. One verse in particular is *Deuteronomy 18:15-19: "The LORD your God will raise up for you a prophet like me from among your own brothers. You must listen to him. For this is what you asked of the LORD your God at Horeb on the day of the assembly when you said, 'Let us not hear the voice of the LORD our God nor see this great fire anymore, or we will die.' The LORD said to me: 'What they say is good. I will raise up for them a prophet like you from among their brothers; I will put my words in his mouth, and he will tell them everything I command him. If anyone does not listen to my words that the prophet speaks in my name, I myself will call him to account.'"*

Mohammed himself strongly indicates that he is the prophet referred to here. See the *Quran; (Suras 2:129, 159; 3:81,164; 7:157)*

As soon as he began to recite the Quran and to preach what he claimed God had revealed to him, he and his small group of followers suffered severe persecution from unbelievers. The persecution grew so fierce that in the year 622 they fled from Makkah to the city of Madinah, some 260 miles to the north. This immigration marks the beginning of the Muslim calendar.

After several years, Mohammed and his followers were able to return to Makkah, where they forgave their enemies. Before Mohammed died at the age of sixty-three, the greater part of Arabia was Muslim, and within a century of his death Islam had spread to Spain in the West and as Far East as China.

Toward the end of his life, Mohammed had several hundred thousand followers of Islam. Thousands prayed with him at the mosque and listened to his sermons. Hundreds of sincere Muslims would find every opportunity to be with him. They would seek his advice for every day problems and listened attentively to the interpretation and application of revealed verses to their situation.

It's reported that Mohammed continued to live a most simple, austere and modest life. He and his family use to go without cooked meals several days at a time, relying only on dates, dried bread and water. During the day he was busy with his duties as head of state, chief justice, commander in chief, arbitrator, instructor, and family man. He was reported to have spent up to two-thirds of every night in prayer and meditation.

The *Hadith (or Sunna)* is a very sacred and important book for Muslims. *Sunna* literally means a way or style of life. As a technical term in Islam, it refers to the way the Prophet Mohammed lived. In particular it refers to the ways and practices he wished Muslims to follow; actions and norms lived out and recommended.

There is a consensus among Islamic scholars that the way of *Sunna* is the way of the *din* (religion). *Sunna* is

WWMD What Would Mohammed Do?

likened to a staircase or a ladder to reach *al-Hagg* (the Truth, one of the names of God). Being like Mohammed, according to Muslims, is the way to be acceptable to Allah.

The same thing is happening among Christians in the Bible belt. There was a large marketing blitz in 1998 and 1999 to promote the sale of shirts, hats, bumper stickers, car tags, etc. with the letters, "WWJD" which stands for, *"What Would Jesus Do?"*

It sounds honorable, but there are probably thousands of interpretations as to what Jesus might do in a given situation; from expressing the anger of cleansing the temple, to the compassion shown a woman caught in adultery.

One can use verses in the Bible to justify any position. Take your pick. It's the convenient and customary way to appease and strengthen ties to the religious club.

Mohammed is not here. *He died many centuries ago.* His body is still in the tomb, therefore, it might be appropriate to speculate and ask, WWMD *"what would Mohammed would do?"*

But according to *the Bible*, the tomb of Jesus is empty! *He has risen* and is alive, ever present, living in the hearts and through the lives of any and all who will receive Him. WWJD, *"What Would Jesus Do" implies that He's not here.*

From the Bible John 10:27:
Jesus says,
   "My sheep listen to my voice; I know them, and they follow me." John 15:5:

Bob McLeod

"I am the Vine. You are the branches. Without Me you can do nothing."

Suppose you are standing with two of your friends. While ignoring you, one asks the other what he thinks you would do in a given situation? And all the while you're standing right there with them! *How would that make you feel?*

Some of the people who wear WWJD paraphernalia are not ignoring Jesus. They simply are doing so in order to share their faith with others.

Mean Religious People

According to the Book *(John 15:12)* Jesus gave one commandment: *"to love one another as I have loved you."* In 1978 Bob Dylan in one of his songs asked an incredibly honest and poignant question directed at Christians: *"You talk about a life of brotherly love. Show me someone who knows how to live it!"*

Let's dare to look at what's called Christian history and *"judge the tree by its fruit."* Jews, Eastern Christians and Muslims were all deeply traumatized and affected by the Crusades. Jews were slaughtered in several places. Eastern Christians (Greek Orthodox and others) were mistreated and humiliated by the Crusader armies, increasing the divisions that already existed. Muslims were killed in great numbers, encouraging centuries of deep hostility.

Many Muslims have a much better memory of the Crusades than Christians do. *"It's another crusade!"* is a phrase that recurs regularly in the rhetoric of some Muslim leaders. Muslim fundamentalists today frequently refer to western culture and economic influence as "the last Crusade." Terrorist groups including Al Qaida have in recent years declared a Jihad (holy war) on Jews and Crusaders.

In 1098, Pope Innocent III *(can you believe that guy was actually called 'innocent!')* proclaimed the Fourth Crusade to be directed at Egypt, believing that would be the key to regaining Jerusalem. The expedition took an unexpected turn, however, and the Pope could not stop it.

The Crusaders gathered at Venice, Italy, but they could not raise enough money to sail to the Holy Land. They made an arrangement with the Venetians. The Crusaders agreed to conquer the Christian City of Zara if the Venetians would take them on to Jerusalem. Pope Innocent III ordered the army not to proceed and even excommunicated them, but he could not stop them.

After conquering Zara, the Crusaders diverted to Constantinople (now Istanbul), the richest Christian city in the world. They plundered the city and took its wealth, including the treasures of the great church Hagia Sophia. They battled against other Christian men and raped Christian women.

Even though other Christians had been transgressed, the Crusaders, who returned with many eastern treasures, generally were not condemned by European society. The so-called Innocent Pope III even removed the ban that had excommunicated them. The acquisition of the Greek Empire was, after all, a great prize.

The Byzantine historian Nicetas Choniates (ca.1155-1216) gave this account of the sack of Constantinople:

"No one escaped the grief. In the alleys, in the streets, in the temples: weeping, lamentations, grief, the groaning of men, the shrieks of women, wounds, rape, captivity, the separation of those most closely united. Nobles wandered about ignominiously; those of venerable age in tears, the rich in poverty. Thus it was in the streets, on the corners, in the temple, in the dens: for no place remained without assault. All places everywhere were filled full of all kinds of crime. Oh, immortal God, how great the afflictions of the men, how great the distress!

It's no wonder that "Christian" is not a very nice word to many people. Why has so much hatred and cruelty surrounded this book we call the Holy Bible, the book some claim is a love letter from God? Historically, Christian terrorists have marched and murdered under the banner of Christ with Bible in hand.

Muslims believe that it was necessary for Allah to send Mohammed and the Quran in order to straighten out the mess made by the "people of the Book." Mahatma Gandhi is quoted as saying that he would have considered becoming a Christian were it not for their history!

A dear friend and pastor, who is also a mental health professional, did an educational internship some years ago in a mental hospital. He told me of a patient there who was constantly pleading for someone to read him the Bible. These lyrics were inspired:

Unholy Lie

In an insane asylum in a dark and lonely room,
An old man cries, "Would someone read me the Bible please!"
The chaplain walks right by him
Through the shadows and the gloom

And leaves the old man all alone, pleading on his knees.
Jesus said, "If your eye offends you, pluck it out."
The old man didn't doubt, he obeyed.
Now the light that God had given him,
He never again will see,
Because, there's only empty sockets where his eyes use to be!
The doer of the Word is so alone and so afraid.

The One Who inspired the writing of the Bible
Must inspire the reading of the Bible
Or else, your Holy Bible is an unholy lie!

The Bible believing Pharisees searched the Scriptures daily
Sharpening their swords, ever ready to condemn.
When God, Himself came to their town,
They gnashed their teeth and put Him down,
Raised their Bible's proudly high and cried, "Crucify Him!"

The One Who inspired the writing of the Bible
Must inspire the reading of the Bible
Or else, your Holy Bible is an unholy lie!

From the Bible:
John 5:39

"You search the Scriptures daily because in them you think you have life, but it's they which testify of Me."

If life were found in knowing "the Book," then our scholars could save us. The deifying of man's intellect has only made him a more clever and vicious devil. There have never been a more educated, dignified, and cultured people than Nazi Germany.

Life is not found in knowing the Book. It is found in knowing the God of the Book. He's the One Who has been, and is being so terribly and grossly misrepresented.

Throughout the course of history, people reacting to the misrepresentation of God have birthed countless religious groups, denominations and militant factions. *There are more demons under haloes than horns!*

Call Him Allah or call Him Abba Father. Even though He's been terribly misrepresented, He remains the same: the One Who loves the people He has created with an unfailing love, a love that will continue to echo throughout all eternity. *"I give My life to forgive and heal you!"*

A man with an experience is not at the mercy of a man with an argument. One who has truly experienced God and His love has no reason to be offended and has nothing to prove in order to validate himself or his God.

Bob McLeod

Freed By His Love

I'm not tied to the emotions of the moment.
I'm not bound by the things that pass away.
I have died;
Nno longer try to make a name or stake a claim.
I've been born from above,
Freed by His love.
I'm not running from anything.
I'm not running for anything.
Got no axe to grind,
Found joy and peace of mind.
I've been born from above.
Freed by His love.

The word "religion" means different things to different people. When I use the word "religion" in this book, I'm referring to *"man's self willed, intolerant, mean and legalistic attempt to play God and control other people."* I'm not talking about the *"ole' time religion"* that Grandma sang about, that makes me love everybody."

Each and every one of the world's religions, whether it is Judaism, Islam, Hinduism, Buddhism or counterfeit Christianity, is saying, in effect, *"You must 'do right' to 'be right'."* That's it in a nutshell. We can spend years studying comparative religions if we want to, but the bottom line is *"do right to be right."* The reason mankind is so frustrated, confused and lonely is because we place demands on ourselves we're not capable of meeting.

The religious conflicts are always over which "do right" is the right "do right" to make one right. *If we could "do right" to "be right" then Christ would not have had to suffer and die!*

Many of our Muslim friends don't recognize Allah's purpose in the sacrificial death of our Lord. Neither do many *"people of the Book."* That's why "do it yourself salvation" is so widespread. The result is always false humility *(guilt, regret and shame) or* self-righteousness (egotism). Both are prevalent in the Bible belt as well as in Muslim countries.

In our neck of the woods there is a popular large sign that hangs in front of the sanctuary of many country Baptist churches called, *"The Church Covenant."* It lists the rules of the religious club, making it very clear what's expected if one is to be in good standing with the church family. It's also very effective in keeping sinners out of the church.

This list of the things to do and not to do has an obvious emphasis on abstaining from alcohol. Quite a few people in our culture associate being saved or lost with alcohol consumption. This definitely doesn't apply to Episcopals, I must add.

Ask a typical good ole' backwoods, Bible-Belt country boy if he's a Christian, and often times he'll drop his head and admit he drinks a bit, or else he'll admit that he used to drink but now he's in church.

This could be why it's reported that alcoholism is more prevalent in the Bible belt than anywhere else on earth. *The forbidden fruit has always been irresistible for fallen man.*

What we're to do and not to do has become the issue rather than the Christ who says, *"It is done; finished!"* The emphasis, so often, is on sin, darkness and death rather than forgiveness, light and life.

He Never Said to Curse the Darkness

Self proclaimed prophets clearing temples of their choice,
Wounding little sheep as all the wolves rejoice.
Claim they hate sin but then, it's everyone's sin, but their own.
How's the sheep gonna to see the Light
When they spend their whole life dodging stones.

He never said to curse the darkness,
We're to let His Light shine.
He never said to put down your neighbor
Or treat this troubled world unkind.
So leave the judging to the judge.
When love is tested, that's when we see that it's really love.
Our Jesus never, ever ridicules the blind.
We can rejoice even in darkness
Because, it's there we can see His Light shine!

We can't look down our nose
At someone else when we're washing their feet,

And that's heart of love that opens blinded eyes to see.
Jesus still eats with sinners.
Today He had lunch with me.
He took all the condemnation away
When He died on Calvary,
And He keeps reminding me.

He never said to Curse the Darkness...

It's also interesting to note the many so-called sins that are not included in the "Church Covenant." There's no mention of gluttony, even though it's the twin brother of drunkenness according to the Book. *(Proverbs 23:21)*

I've also noticed that the Church Covenant makes no reference to the sins of worry, gossip, adultery, resentment, pornography or sexual perversion, all of which are being practiced by a growing number of respectable church folk in the Bible belt.

According to the Book *(John 8:32)* the truth will make one free. If this is accurate, then why are so many people of the Book in bondage? Selfish ambition, worry, fear, jealousy, anger, and lust bind so many. The Book says that we can know a tree by its fruit. Could it be that a lot of what we call 'Christian' is a counterfeit?

Bob McLeod

Christianity is The Disguise
2 Corinthians 11:14,15

He prowls about like a roaring lion,
Disguising himself as an angel of light.
Such charisma, oh, what a brilliant mind.
The wolf is in sheep's clothing
But the people, they don't even know him
    'Cause they've lost their sight.
He says, "You can't be saved until we baptize you.
To get to God you've got to go through me.
Let me interpret the Bible for you
Or else you're going to spend your life in Hell throughout eternity.
Come let me set you free!"

The sheep are slowly led to slaughter.
Look at the admiration in their eyes.
They even sacrifice their sons and their daughters
    'Cause it's not Jesus, it's the preacher that they idolize,

Christianity is The Disguise.
Christianity is The Disguise.

Religion is deadly because it's centered upon imperfect man's efforts to be perfect, rather than being centered on a perfect God Who has made a way to perfect us. Our part is to receive.

WWMD What Would Mohammed Do?

Jesus cried, "It is finished." He did not cry, *"To be continued."* We can add nothing to that. *You can read about it in the Book.*

Bob McLeod

Mother Nature Kills Muslims and Christians

It's been said that tragedy introduces a man to himself. Just as a black velvet backdrop heightens the sparkle and beauty of a precious gem, what we call tragedy allows us to see the living Jesus much more clearly! Tim and I were very touched as we saw the reality of the risen Christ shining through a small group of people in a city called Izmit. Here's an account of what happened to these people only a year before:

"It was the early morning hours of August 17, 1999. Everybody was asleep on the vacationing coastline of Izmit Bay near the big city of Istanbul, Turkey. Local vacationers and foreign tourists, who came from big cities like Ankara, Istanbul and remote places like the US and Israel, were enjoying the summer and beautiful beeches of Marmara. They had come with their children and grandchildren. Some were retired. Some were in the best years of their professions. All the local towns and villages around the bay were in deep quiet. All of a sudden at 3:02 a.m. the earth started shaking very violently. One of the deadliest earthquakes of the Twentieth Century had begun. This earthquake lasted for exactly forty-five seconds. According to surveys more than 30,000 were killed and more than 100,000 badly injured. 300,000 to 400,000 became homeless."

We were privileged to worship the Lord Jesus Christ with some of the survivors in a small church that was meeting in an attic. The people's faces were aglow with the eternal hope they had found in our risen Savior. Thank God for the missionaries He sent to offer these people His gift of comfort and eternal life!

While we were there in Izmit, my mind went back to Palm Sunday, 1994, when a violent tornado ripped through our home community killing many of our friends. Once again, we experienced the Lord Jesus Christ and His very personal love and care.

This particular tragedy allowed us to see the dramatic contrast between those who have a relationship with Christ and those whose Christianity is a cruel, legalistic counterfeit.

Palm Sunday is the Sunday before Easter. Christians recognize this day each year to remember when Christ came into Jerusalem to be crucified.

I was serving as interim pastor at Nances Creek Baptist Church, located just south of Piedmont, Alabama. In preparation for the upcoming Palm Sunday service and sermon, I spent the entire week reflecting upon the heartbreak that comes from living on this planet, the trauma of being human and, in particular, the sorrow, grief, and agony experienced by the man, Jesus.

My research included a 1986 article from the Journal of the American Medical Association, entitled, *"On the Physical Death of Jesus Christ."* This article was written by a team of medical doctors and describes in excruciating detail what happens to someone who is being crucified.

Jesus was publicly stripped. His muscles and skin were literally shred apart by metal and bone-tipped whips. He was completely exhausted from lack of sleep and no food. The endless hours of intense interrogation, ruthless public ridicule and humiliation, heightened His distress and torment. Jesus' forehead was pierced and sliced by a needle-sharp crown of thorns.

The article goes on to describe what really happens to a human body when it's nailed and hung to a rugged, splintered, wooden cross: the dislocation of joints, collapse of the lungs, a ruptured heart and death confirmed by a sword run through the side. This torture causes the body to writhe in agonizing convulsions and all the while insects light upon or burrow into the open wounds as well as the ears, eyes and nose of the dying victim. Birds of prey also tear at these sites. Whatever the degree of one's suffering, it will never surpass or be more horrible, excruciating and agonizing than that of this man, Jesus Christ.

Palm Sunday 1994 arrived. The Bible text for the sermon included *1 John 2:17: "And the world is passing away, and also its lusts; but the one who does the will of God abides forever."* The sermon reminded us that everything physical is temporary. Our heartbeat is simply the ticking of a little clock counting down our brief time in this earth.

In addition to this sobering reminder, we also began to see a very definite but often over-looked quality and expression of authentic love; that is, the experience of shared suffering. Just as the crucifixion and suffering of Jesus soon ended, our suffering is also "for a moment" and is to be shared. There is powerful healing in shared suffering!

During our service, at precisely 11:32 a.m., the electricity in the church suddenly went off. In order to have more light, I moved toward a window and continued preaching. We had no idea that there was a tornado warning.

Usually our services left us inspired, and filled with joy and hope. This Palm Sunday was different. There was an unusual atmosphere of sadness, sorrow and even despair.

Little did we know that at that precise hour, just a few miles north of us, our friends and family at the Goshen Valley United Methodist Church were being mercilessly slaughtered and massacred by a violent tornado. Seven of those being killed were children.

This is an entry from my journal the week that followed: "This week the reality of shared suffering is in our face! Last week it was more like a theory, philosophy or another sermon topic. This week it's painfully real. We are hurting and crying with our neighbors. The burden is so heavy! We feel so helpless and, in a way, everything seems so hopeless."

We're haunted by the sounds of "if only!" If only a warning had been heard! If only our friends had not been in church! If only they'd found cover! Oh, the haunting hopelessness of those words, "if only!"

There's so much visible destruction. Large, massive, solid physical structures have crumbled and disintegrated, as if they were made of matchsticks.

Bob McLeod

The pain we feel, however, is not from the loss of material possessions. Homes and churches can be rebuilt. Trees can be replanted. Power lines can be restored. The real heartbreak and agony is the vivid memory of the precious people who aren't with us any more. We'll never hug them again. We'll never see them smile again. We once heard the laughter of children, but now there is deathly silence, broken only by the sobs of those who remain.

Being a tornado victim is like being savagely raped. A vicious and merciless monster comes tearing through for only a few seconds, rips apart that which is most sacred and precious to us; then leaves in its trail, shattered dreams, broken lives, and despicable human carnage. It's as if he vents his wrath and anger and then disappears without any consideration of who we are and what we've lost.

We're desperate to forever stop this monster. We have our own rage and anger to vent toward him. But we can't. We're helpless. We can't retaliate. We can't sue him. It's as if he's gone, but is yet quietly waiting in the shadows of what we perceive to be nowhere, perched and waiting to strike again one day when we least expect it.

His brief but devastating visit has deeply engraved in our hearts a painful and excruciating memory—a memory that could very easily curse our lives forever with a lingering and prevailing sense of dread and fear.

Piedmont, Alabama and the surrounding area will have twenty-two funeral services this week. The hospital medical staffs are treating people who are emotionally and physically broken, devastated and suffering from a pain that morphine can't even begin to touch.

I wonder why this Thursday before Easter is so beautiful. The Dogwood Trees are in full bloom. The sun is bright. The sky is crystal clear and blue. The birds are singing. Doesn't nature know what happened only a few days ago? How can it be so dark one day and bright the next?

Is this Mother Nature who is blessing us with such beauty and life today, the same one who was murdering our loved ones and children only a few days ago? Is she that sinister? It's as if she's mocking us! She sends storm clouds to kill us and then sun to shine on us as we bury our dead!

In an attempt not to deny the Christian claims and faith, people have been heard trying to explain: "God loves us. He's not responsible for this!" It's Mother Nature's fault. They were in the wrong place at the wrong time." When I hear this kind of religious rhetoric, I can't help but wonder, can't Father control mother?

I also hear voices that have become very familiar in the Bible belt: the unmerciful, heartless and judgmental voices of religious cruelty. "That Methodist Church where all those people were killed had a woman preacher! They were living in rebellion to the Word of God that says in *1 Timothy 2:12* and other places that women are to remain silent in church. God got tired of it and His judgment came on them! They had sin in their lives. That's why God's wrath came!"

I can't help but wonder, "How did they miss reading about Esther, Phoebe, Mary, Joel's prophecy of daughters who will prophesy and all the other wonderful, powerfully used women of the Bible? What hope can there be in that narrow-minded mentality? And again I'm reminded of the human cruelty and heartbreak that's been justified by man's tunnel-vision interpretation of the Bible! Some people obviously read an "Unholy Bible!" Man's religious arguments and self-righteous judgments have never offered a solution or a valid explanation for life, suffering and death.

Free From The Pharisee

He came walking right up to me,
Smug and self-righteous,
Looked just like he swallowed a curtain rod.
Squeezed his Old Testament,
The dude thought he was heaven-sent.
He said he came to get me right with God,
And all you other infidels who are headin'
Straight to hell,
He said to pray with him,
Then he'd show us what else to do.
I said, "Sir, before you go,
There's one thing I want to know.
If I get saved,
Will it make me like you?"
The tail keeps waggin' the dog.
Have you ever seen such a sight?
Some men profess to be men of God
And God only knows that's not right.

The tail keeps waggin' the dog,
Legalism to the core.
The law is for man
Not man for the law
And Jesus set us free from the law
Forever more!

Many of us have been taught since childhood not to question God. We're to walk by faith, accept things as they come, and never ask why. I'm sorry. Deep inside of me there's an angry, frightened little boy who feels so betrayed, so alone, and so grieved with the loss and suffering around us, that I want to stand up and scream out to the Heavens with everything that is within me, "Why God? Why? Why?"

Does omnipotent mean all-powerful? If God is God, He must have all power, right? Then this destruction has to be His fault! We teach our children to sing, "He's got the wind and the rain in His hands" and then, the wind and the rain kill them! Why God?

Some people blame the devil. I'm sure the devil enjoys the credit and attention, but is the devil God? If not, then who gives him the right and the power to kill God's children?

I know. Maybe the pragmatic atheists are right when they say, "there is no God! Everything is by chance. Christians are naïve, superstitious fools. Last Saturday night some immoral, God defying, hell-raisers left the strip joint and went home drunk and laughing with somebody else's wife. While they were safely tucked away in their warm, soft, comfortable beds, sleeping through a hangover, the Christians who were worshipping their make-believe God got slaughtered! Let's hear the so-called God-fearing people explain that!"

It seems that, since there's a creation, there has to be a creator. But if there really is a God, how can anyone like Him, much less love Him? He'd have to be some kind of vicious monster! Life on earth is the epitome of cruelty. The Palm Sunday massacre proves that!

"Where is your God now?" the atheist asks. Does anyone have an answer? We're looking for a real answer, not some pious cover-up for a religion that's nothing more than a vehicle for greedy, self-seeking, ambitious clergy to sell their desensitizing opiate to the people. Can anyone make any sense of this?

And then, right in the midst of my despair, confusion and hopelessness, my mind drifts back many years ago to an old country church house on a sweltering summer day. I'm a small, restless little boy snuggled next to my grandmother. Her arm is around me. I can smell the fragrance of her powder and perfume. I can feel the gentle breezes from the wooden handle "funeral home" fan she's using to cool me as she swishes in time with the old upright piano. I can see her look down at me and gently smile as she sings,

> "On a hill far away stood an old rugged cross,
> The emblem of suffering and shame;
> And I love that Old Cross where the dearest and best
> For a world of lost sinners was slain."

What was that cross all about? Who was that man? Was He really God? Why did He come? Why did He share man's suffering to such an extreme? Wasn't He innocent? What was He saying to us?

Could the horrible events of this Palm Sunday be a continuation of His suffering? Does He continue to share the suffering of humanity? If so, then why? Could He really love us that much?

And what about Easter? What about the resurrection? Since He shares our suffering, could it be that we can share His resurrection? Of course! That's it! God is identifying with us "in the temporal" so that we can identify with Him "in the eternal."

The clouds are clearing now. Light is breaking through. The very essence and meaning of our existence is beginning to unfold. His Spirit is here. He's guiding us in all truth, just like He said He would. He's comforting us, consoling us, and giving us peace. He's filling us with a renewed hope, coming from an awareness of eternal life and love. Somehow we're able to know that, though we suffer, we don't suffer in vain. Every Calvary has a resurrection!

From the Bible:
2 Corinthians 4:17
"For our light affliction, which is but for a moment, worketh for us a far more exceeding and eternal weight of glory"

Bob McLeod

Romans 8:18
"I consider that our present sufferings are not worth comparing with the glory that will be revealed in us."

Death and destruction are not God's fault. They are the result of our rebellion against Him. We left Him. He didn't leave us. The creature rebelled against the Creator, but the Creator couldn't leave His creatures without a way. The innocent, spotless Lamb of God came into the Earth; He suffered, bled and died, not only to identify with our self-imposed suffering and death, but also to demonstrate His love for us by declaring to the high court of the Universe on our behalf: pardoned!

John 3:16
"For God so loved the world that He gave His only Begotten Son, that whosoever believeth in Him should not perish but have everlasting life."

This complete forgiveness paved the way for us to intimately identify with His righteousness.

2 Corinthians 5:21
"For he hath made him to be sin for us, who knew no sin; that we might be made the righteousness of God in him."

When Billy (there's that name again) Clinton was running for President of the United States, he hung a large sign on the wall of his campaign headquarters. The sign was the focal point of the room, a constant reminder to all of his campaign staff. The sign read, **"THE ECONOMY STUPID!"** In other words, if we're to win this election we've got to stay focused on the economy. It worked. Governor Clinton became President Clinton.

It might do well for us to place large signs in our churches, homes, schools, and places of business, which read: **"ETERNAL LIFE STUPID!"**

If our point of reference is this temporary, physical place that is passing away, then any semblance of hope will be merely a fool's dream. If our point of reference is eternity, then our hope will be real and we can pass through any storm unscathed.

The Bible:
Colossians 3:2
  "Set your mind on things above, not on Earthly things."

To him who looks below, life is a tragedy. To him who looks above, life is a comedy!

Our communities have come together in an incredibly special way. We have shared each other's suffering. A bonding has taken place that is the cement of eternal love. It's happening, not in spite of the tragedy, but because of it. Jesus is alive. He's here. Everything is going to be okay, eternally okay!

Some of our Methodist friends and their children went to church on Palm Sunday to worship Jesus and remember His suffering. The service was incredibly precious and special for them. They began to see the Lord Jesus Christ face to face! They were welcomed through the portals of Heaven and joined the saints of the ages and the myriad of angels surrounding the throne of Almighty God. They were allowed to enter into the high praise, honor and adoration of our glorious King Jesus, Who reins forever and forever!

What a joy to know that we're right behind them. The clocks are ticking away. The time is approaching when we'll be reunited with our loved ones, and our faith will end in sight. Easter is coming! Easter is coming!

Those in that little congregation who remained with us, gathered together on a beautiful and bright Easter Sunday Morning. Many were bandaged, arms in slings, some limping on crutches, several being pushed in their wheel chairs. They assembled in front of where their church building stood only a few days before.

There, in the presence of international reporters and an assortment of major network TV Cameras, they unashamedly and courageously sang this Bill Gaither classic to the world:

> *"Because He lives I can face tomorrow.*
> *Because he lives all fear is gone.*
> *I know Who holds the future*
> *And life is worth the living*
> *Just because He lives!"*

What's that sound in the distance? It's getting louder and louder. It's beautiful. I'm beginning to feel the joy! What is

WWMD What Would Mohammed Do?

it? Who is it? Of course, it's the children. Yes, the children. Oh thank God! Do you hear them? They're laughing! Easter is coming! Easter is coming!

Bob McLeod

The Five Pillars

Bob McLeod

Introducing The Five Pillars

1 Corinthians 4:7
*"For who makes you different from anyone else? What do you have that you did not **receive**? And if you did **receive** it, why do you boast as though you did not?"*

John 1:12
*"Yet to all who **received** him, to those who believed in his name, he gave the right to become children of God—"*

We get nothing from God except that which we *receive*. This one simple declaration is the key to understanding the "how to" of unconditional love. It's also the key to escaping the self centered, deadly and tragic consequences of legalism.

In order to be in a position to receive love, we must first recognize and admit how destitute and helpless we are. This is a deathblow to pride and self-sufficiency.

Legalism says, *"I must do right to be right."*
Truth says:
*"I don't do right to be right.
I do right because I am right.
I am right because He's making me right.
He's making me right because
I humble my heart before Him
And receive His love."*

Love is a free gift. To try and earn love by self-effort is to reject the gift! The result is always fear, insecurity, loneliness, restlessness and a fractured, negative self-image. We humans were designed to be recipients and expressions of our Creator's love. When we reject love, we reject the very reason for our existence. Our world is dying from a love famine simply because we're too independent and prideful to receive. Most of us are either striving for success in order to prove ourselves or else we're giving up entirely, often times even committing suicide.

Muslims interpret the message of God through what are called the five pillars of Islam. Mohammed underlined them in his last address at Arafat.

The five pillars are quite simply the Muslim's *"do right to be right"* list. Many so-called Christians have their own *"do right to be right"* lists. They just aren't as obvious, and they differ according to denomination. This includes the denomination that boasts in being non-denominational.

As we look at Islam's Five Pillars, we will also look at how certain traditional Christians adopt them *sub silentio*, doing exactly the same thing as they strive to "do" rather than to "be."

Love With a Hook

He found her note on the pillow on their bed.
"I don't love you anymore" was all she said.

WWMD What Would Mohammed Do?

How do you tell a little girl that her Mommy is gone?
When her Mommy's last words were, "I love you, so long."
Love with a hook in it is not love at all.

Lucre Christian Chapel was named in Phil T's honor
'Cause Dr. Phil T. Lucre was the church's biggest donor.
And every time Phil T. disagreed with what the preacher said,
The preacher had to leave.
Now Lucre Christian Chapel is dead.
Love with a hook in it is not love at all.

A man speaks peace to his neighbor but in his heart
He's setting an ambush to move in like a killer shark.
A wolf in sheep's clothing, flattering words disguise,
Leave unsuspecting souls bleeding, brutalized.
Love with a hook in it is not love at all.

They knock at your door with a handshake and a track.
Ask you if you know Jesus, then leave in their new Cadillac.
No food in the cupboard, the baby's sick and it's a wonder.
Their hidden agenda was nickels, noses and numbers.
Love with a hook in it is not love at all.

"Father forgive them," we hear Love cry.
"They know not what they do."
Then we see Love die.

Bob McLeod

Pillar One: Shahada, *a simple statement*

The first pillar of Islam is the *shahada*. It is a simple statement declaring belief and bearing witness in the one God and Mohammad as his messenger. This declaration is the only requirement for a person to become a Muslim.

The counterpart to the *shahada* in the American Bible Belt is called the *"sinner's prayer."* A so-called lost person (non-Christian) is led in a simple "repeat after me" prayer something to this effect:

"God, I know I'm a sinner. Thank you for sending Jesus to die on the cross for me. Jesus, please come into my heart and save me. Amen."

The Bible-belt evangelist is an itinerate preacher who goes from church to church preaching evangelistic crusades. Often, but certainly not always, the number of people the visiting evangelist can coerce into praying this prayer in front of others determines his success and popularity.

Usually, the evangelistic appeal is at the end of a service and is emotionally charged with threats of *"you may die any moment"* and the reality of hell. There is also an emphasis on coming forward publicly. This is vital if the evangelist is to build his reputation and get more meetings in other churches. It helps him protect his livelihood and it also adds people to the church roll, which in turn helps the home pastor maintain his livelihood.

There are certainly people who respond to the invitation and are converted as they pray the sinner's prayer, but very often, that's not the case. The deadly deception here is that making a statement or praying a prayer will save someone when in reality, it won't. This is one reason there are so many disillusioned, disinterested, tormented so-called Christians.

It's also why many seekers of truth will not go near a church. All they see is manipulation and exploitation and they want no part of it.

The acceptable, American Bible Belt way to Heaven is to pray the prayer, usually in an emotional moment, go through the baptismal waters and get your name on a church roll. Baptists call this, "Getting Your Letter." Seldom is the message the one Jesus preached: *"Surrender ALL and follow me."*

Many times families cling to a pet doctrine called *"Once saved, always saved"* in hopes that no matter how evil their loved one becomes, he'll go to Heaven when he dies, all because he prayed the prayer one day. It's a terrible, tragic deception with a never-ending, most horrible consequence. The sinner's prayer is nothing but words unless there is a heart change.

They Call it Repentance"

The evangelist comes to town.
He says for Christ's sake.
The more the people cry,
The more money in the collection plate.

Bob McLeod

> *Kleenex at the altar,*
> *Screamin' and cryin' a lot,*
> *They called it repentance,*
> *But it's snot!*
>
> *Thank God, it's okay to cry,*
> *Even laugh when you've been set free,*
> *But feelings come and feelings go*
> *Like the waves of a shallow sea.*
>
> *When there's no heart change,*
> *Every thing remains the same,*
> *They may call it repentance, but it's not!*

A number of years ago I read a letter in the Alabama Baptist, a denominational newspaper, praising a powerful, young, charismatic evangelist. *"One of the greatest preachers of our time, bringing hundreds of young people into the saving knowledge of Jesus Christ,"* it said.

I was invited to share one Wednesday night in a local church. We had to meet in the fellowship hall because of construction in the main sanctuary. The Sunday before, this young evangelist had preached there. There were so many people at the altar the floor caved in!

A week or so later I went to one of his meetings. The atmosphere was charged with a sense of excitement and anticipation. The presence of God seemed so intense. This *"fire ball"* preacher mesmerized everyone in the building, including myself.

After a few hymns and a solo, with Bible in hand, the man of God approached the pulpit. I couldn't help but recall the lyrics of the Neil Diamond classic,

Brother Love's Travelin' Salvation Show:

*"The room gets suddenly still and when you'll almost bet
You can hear yourself sweat, he walks in...
Eyes black as coal,
And when he lifts his face every ear in the place is on him,
Starts soft and slow like a small earthquake,
Then when he lets go
Half the valley shakes!"*

The young evangelist seemed to stalk the congregation, as he'd pace back and forth across the platform, gaining intensity with every breath and word. His eyes blazed like a red-hot steel sword just pulled from the blacksmith's furnace. He angrily stomped his foot, pointed his finger and screamed at the crowd, *"Jesus is coming back soon! You better get right or get left!"*

Then, as his hell fire, brim stone sermon began to conclude, he paused for a moment and demanded, *"Every head bowed and every eye closed."*

He waited for several minutes, then broke the deathly silence with a stern and emotional appeal: *"While no one is watching, if you don't want to go to hell, then raise your hand."* I sure did raise my hand but I don't know how many others did. I was afraid to look. There must have been many others, for he kept saying, *"God bless you. God bless you."* I suppose it was his acknowledgment of those who were raising their hands.

He then began to threaten the ones who didn't respond. *"The rest of you have a one way ticket to hell!"* he screamed. At that point he had everyone stand. *"If you raised your hand then come down to this altar."*

He kept quoting the words of Jesus: *"If you're ashamed of me publicly, then I'll be ashamed of you before my Father!"*

"Are you ashamed of Jesus? If so, then be a coward, stay where you are and go to hell!" He threatened.

The altar began filling with people crying and screaming! Counselors approached and began filling out cards, counting and recording the many *"professions of faith."* I quietly slipped out the back door and went home, wondering why I was so grieved even to the point of being nauseated.

The following week I read in the local newspaper where this *"fast becoming a celebrity"* evangelist had been pulled over in his new sports car and arrested for possession of cocaine. He was in such a rage that the police had to restrain him and lock him in an isolated, padded cell.

I met with him shortly after his release from jail. He was so broken, remorseful and humbled.

"I've always had a gift to gab." He said. "I was a king pin drug dealer in another state when I attended an evangelistic meeting. I went to the altar and *'prayed the prayer.'*

Since I had such a bad reputation, the preachers loved for me to give my testimony. People would respond and I began to have more invitations to churches than I could accept. And there was money in it. Instead of selling dope, I was selling my testimony!

I didn't know the Bible. I didn't even know God, but I could manipulate people and make the preachers look good. *Bob, I didn't meet Jesus until I was alone with Him in that jail!"*

Bob McLeod

Pillar Two: Salat, *praying*

The second pillar of Islam is prayer. Salat is the name for the obligatory prayers, which are performed five times a day and are a direct link between the worshipper and God.

There is no official hierarchical authority in Islam; however, the congregation chooses a learned person who seems to know the Quran to lead in the prayers. These five prayers contain verses from the Quran, and are said in Arabic, the language of the Revelation, but personal supplication can be offered in one's own language.

Prayers are said at dawn, noon, mid-afternoon, sunset and nightfall, and thus determine the rhythm of the entire day. Although it is preferable to worship together in a mosque, a Muslim may pray almost anywhere, such as in fields, offices, factories or schools. Visitors to the Muslim world are often impressed by the dedication and centrality of prayers in daily life.

The translation of the call to prayer is:

> *God is most great. God is most great.*
> *God is most great. God is most great.*
> *I testify that there is no god except Allah.*
> *I testify that there is no god except Allah.*
> *I testify that Mohammed is the messenger of God.*
> *I testify that Mohammed is the messenger of God.*
> *Come to prayer. Come to prayer.*

Come to success (in this life and the hereafter)!
Come to success! God is most great.
God is most great. There is no god except Allah.

American Bible-Belt Christians also place an emphasis on prayer, typically before meals, and at the beginning and end of worship services in the local churches. Wednesday night is often referred to as the *"midweek prayer meeting."*

In the more reserved churches, various needs of the community are discussed and one member will be called upon to voice a single prayer for the entire congregation.

In some churches, however, only God knows what the people are praying. They begin to pray out loud (and I do mean "loud!") all at the same time. The sound is unusual, like the roar of rushing waters. It begins to intensify like an approaching locomotive gaining speed. At the peak of the crescendo people will sometime fall, weeping with shouts of "A-man and A-man!" Sometimes the roar will be seasoned with an unintelligible sound known as *"tongues."*

Many churches have waged war with each other and angrily split over the issue of speaking in tongues. It's very controversial in the Bible belt.

Many Pentecostals, also known by some as *"Holy Rollers,"* believe that speaking in tongues is a demonstration of the spirituality of a brother or sister. *"Getting' the Baptism"* is a term used for being filled with the Holy Ghost. *"If you don't speak in tongues then you ain't got the Baptism!"* some claim.

There's another religion that is perhaps the most prominent in the Bible belt and throughout America. The public demonstration of prayer is exactly the same as Muslims bowing toward Mecca. But instead of Mecca, representatives of the crowd (cheerleaders) bow toward steel upright posts, praying, as one of their gods tries to kick a bag full of zipped-up air through them. If the young god wants to remain a god, then he must kick the bag of air successfully.

This popular religion called football requires public human sacrifices. Though there are some deaths, the sacrifices usually aren't fatal, just very painful and debilitating. The young men go through a bloody, violent ritual in order to appease the crowd and become one of their gods. The crowd fails to recognize, that if photographs were taken of the young men's bodies following a worship service, it would be admissible evidence in their courts for child abuse or assault.

The University of Alabama football team has historically been referred to as the *"Crimson Tide."* I guess the crimson refers to blood, but I'm not sure.

Glory to the Crimson Tide

As they bow their knees praying for another extra point,
The huge crowd roars and leaps to its feet.
The screaming can be heard throughout planet earth,
Carried through the air by NBC.

And all night long they'll celebrate another victory for the Tide.
It's all they'll talk about for another week.
So caught up in the drunken spirit, screams and frantic cheers
That they can't hear the still small voice, who speaks,
Saying, "Come, all of you who labor and are heavy laden
And I'll give you rest just to ease your troubled soul.
Let My Spirit take you high, give you joy and peace untold
And open your eyes to the Crimson Tide that will forever roll!"
Can't you see 'um, fillin' up the Roman Coliseum,
Slowly dying in what they call their Sugar Bowl.
And all the while, the real Crimson Tide just keeps rolling
From a hill called Calvary.
He's giving life to some but to others, just a stumbling block.
The real Crimson Tide will roll forever but here on planet earth
It's late in the forth and no one can stop the clock.
Glory to the Crimson Tide!
The Crimson Blood is cleansing us and it's coming in like a tide
And the gates of hell will never prevail again.
He's giving us a choice. We can be on the winning side
But those who refuse to lay their idols down will slowly die in their sin.
Can't you see 'um, filling up the Roman Coliseum
Slowly dying in what they call their Sugar Bowl.

Bob McLeod

Pillar Three: Zakat, *giving*

The third pillar of Islam is the 'Zakat.' One of the most important principals of Islam is that all things belong to God; therefore, human beings hold that wealth in trust. The word, 'Zakat' means both 'purification' and 'growth.' Possessions are purified by setting aside a proportion for those in need and, like the pruning of plants, this cutting back balances and encourages new growth.

Each Muslim calculates his or her own Zapata individually. For most purposes, this involves the payment each year of two-and-a-half percent of one's capital.

A pious person may also give as much as he or she pleases. This is called, sadaqa, and is done preferably in secret. Although this word can be translated as *'voluntary charity'* it has a wider meaning. The Prophet Mohammed said, "*Even meeting your brother with a cheerful face is charity.*"

Mohammed also said, *"Charity is a necessity for every Muslim."* When asked: *"What if a person has nothing?"* He replied, *"He should work with his own hands for his benefit and then give something out of such earnings to charity."*

The companions asked, *"What if he is not able to work?"* Mohammed said, *"He should help the poor and needy persons."*

The companions further asked, *"What if he cannot do even that?"* Mohammed said, *"He should urge others to do good."*

The companions said again, *"What if he lacks that also?"* Mohammed said, *"He should check himself from doing evil. That also is charity."*

The financial *"do right to be right"* in America and the Bible-Belt is called "tithes and offerings." The tithe is 10% of gross income and the offering is any amount above that. Being a good Muslim is a lot less expensive than being a good Christian! These verses from *the Book* are the most frequently used to demand money:

Malachi 3

8 Will a man rob God? Yet ye have robbed me. But ye say, wherein have we robbed thee? In tithes and offerings.

9 Ye are cursed with a curse: for ye have robbed me, even this whole nation.

10 Bring ye all the tithes into the storehouse, that there may be meat in mine house, and prove me now herewith, saith the LORD of hosts, if I will not open you the windows of heaven, and pour you out a blessing, that there shall not be room enough to receive it.

11 And I will rebuke the devourer for your sakes, and he shall not destroy the fruits of your ground; neither shall your vine cast her fruit before the time in the field, saith the LORD of hosts.

The *"out of context"* implication is that God is like a cosmic vending machine. Put in some money and He will *"rebuke the devourer"* and *prosper you*. If you send money, you and/or your sick loved one will be healed and you can get whatever you think you need. If you don't put your money in the cosmic vending machine, then you get cursed! It's a totally self-centered, manipulative ploy. It's not Christ-centered. The slot in the cosmic vending machine is whatever organization is making the appeal.

One of the high priests of country music Hank Williams Jr. made an honest observation and expressed it in one of his songs, *"The preacher says, "Send your money to God, then he gives you his address."*

Healing
1 John 5:21

Cancel all your health insurance.
Muster up your faith for assurance.
Go ahead and claim that your migraine ain't real.
Blacklist the family physician.
Curse the devil for your sick condition.
'Cause Jesus don't sleep on the job and you need to be healed.

Some folks care more about healin' than they care about Jesus.
They got the cart out in front of the horse
And it's distortin' their view.
Some folks care more about healin' than they care about Jesus.
They say, "Heal me Lord, Fill me Lord, give me Lord,
Bless me Lord, make me brand new.

Ain't that the least you can do?"

Well He died to save the sick.
He died to save the healthy as well.
He didn't die to try to glorify flesh
When it's the soul that's a headed for hell.
To escape we gotta give Him our lives, return what's rightfully His.
Do you love Him cause of what He can do for you
Or do you love Him cause of who He is?

A person can be seduced by the Cosmic vending Machine Religion one of two ways. The first is to buy into the lie. The second, which is far more subtle, is to have contempt for those who are deceived into preaching the lie. We must not personally judge the person even though their behavior is obviously demented. We must leave the judging to the Judge, the One before Whom we all must stand.

From the Bible:
Philippians. 1:18
The Apostle Paul says,
   "But what does it matter? The important thing is that in every way, whether from false motives or true, Christ is preached. And because of this I rejoice. Yes, and I will continue to rejoice."

Bob McLeod

Jesus is so merciful and so gracious. He still meets the needs of humble, hurting people, even in the midst of all the religious counterfeits.

It's Not What You Do
1 Peter 2:4-9

G. Howard R. Good gave a hundred thousand dollars
To build a boy's club for the kids on the other side of the tracks.
He was voted man of the year, got the keys to the city,
But it's really such a pity,
All he cared about was savin' on his income tax.
It's not what ya do; it's why you do it,

And it's not what ya say; it's why you say it,
And it's not what's on your face that counts,
It's what's in your heart. It's not who you pretend to be,
It's a Who You Really Are.

Rev. I.M. Slick gets his hair done every Friday
To look his best for all his fans who watch him on TV.
His church is overflowin', got a condo on the ocean,
Praises God and slick promotion for his manufactured popularity.
Judgment day is comin', when all will be known,
Every secret will be told and every motive will be shown.
All the prestige, fame and status will all be burned away.

WWMD What Would Mohammed Do?

And we'll stand before Jesus and this is what He'll say:

"What did you do, why did you do it?
What did you say, why did you say it?
Tell me, what's that on your face?
Is that what's in your heart?
Forget who you pretended to be,
Now let's look at Who You Really Are".

Bob McLeod

Pillar Four: The Fast, *self denial*

The fourth Pillar of Islam is the fast. Every year, in the month of Ramadan, all good Muslims fast from first light until sundown, abstaining from food, drink, and sexual relations. Those who are sick, elderly, or on a journey are exempt. So are pregnant or nursing mothers, providing they make up an equal number of days later in the year. If they are physically unable to do this, they must feed a needy person for every day missed. Children begin to fast (and to observe the prayer) from puberty, although many start earlier.

Although the fast is most beneficial to one's health, it is regarded principally as a method of self-purification. By cutting oneself off from worldly comforts, even for a short period of time, Muslims claim that a fasting person will gain true sympathy with those who go hungry, as well as grow in one's spiritual life.

Any form of conscious self-denial is foreign to most American Bible-Belt Christians. The Catholics do however give up something for lent as a part of Holy week. The Seventh Day Adventists also practice abstinence from certain foods, and some of their women even fast from cosmetics on Saturdays.

Some years ago, I was introduced to a successful, Christian businessman who lived in another city. He and I spent several hours together one Saturday as he described to me the heartbreak and trauma he was going through. He and his wife were childhood friends, they grew up together, went to Bible school together and even served on the foreign mission field together for a number of years.

He was an elder in the Seventh Day Adventist Church and she was a teacher. They had two young children and seemed to be a model family. You can imagine the shock when he discovered that his wife was having an affair with their pastor. She divorced her husband, married the pastor and moved to another city, leaving this man to care for their children.

After our visit this Christian businessman invited me to share with his church. I've never seen a more confused, embarrassed, betrayed and wounded congregation. My wife Patti and I met with them on a Saturday (the actual Sabbath) and we ate a bland, vegetarian lunch with them following the service.

I noticed several of the women were indignantly staring at Patti. I wondered why, and then it dawned on me. Patti was the only one wearing earrings and make up! I also noticed that the women who were staring at her had holes in their ear lobes!

One of the doctrines of the Seventh day Adventists is called, *"the annihilation of the soul"*, which means that when an evil person dies, they cease to exist. They believe that there is no judgment and there is no hell.

The Bible says in *Proverbs 16:6* that *"the fear of God keeps one from evil."* Obviously the adulterous pastor and his mistress, the elder's wife embraced their doctrine. If there's no fear of God and judgment, then why not give into lust?

Bob McLeod

From the Bible:
Hebrews 9:27: 27
   "*Just as man is destined to die once, and after that to face judgment…*"

If I have not personally received God's forgiveness, then, in all likelihood, I will be subconsciously attempting to alleviate my guilt by punishing myself. I may call it fasting or spiritual discipline but in reality, I'm trying to be my own Savior through my self-denial. It may give me a superficial sense of righteousness for a season, but the ultimate outcome is always tragic: I will be constantly sabotaging my own success, never able to shed the torment of guilt, shame and regret, and will always feel unworthy of any joy and happiness.

If I am subconsciously punishing myself, then I'm no different than the group of religious fanatics of the Middle Ages called the flagellants. Clergy and laity, men and women, even children of tender years, scourged themselves in reparation for the sins of the whole world. Great processions, amounting sometimes to ten thousand souls, passed through the towns. Stripped to the waist and with covered faces, they scourged themselves with leather thongs until the blood ran, chanting hymns and canticles of the Passion of Christ, entering churches and prostrating themselves before the altars.

There is only one sacrifice that can remove our guilt and that sacrifice was made at Calvary two thousand years ago:

WWMD What Would Mohammed Do?

From the Bible:
2 Corinthians 5:21
"God made him who had no sin to be sin for us, so that in him we might become the righteousness of God.

Forgive Me
Romans 7

The guilt, regret, the shame and the pain.
Bound by a lie until Your truth came.
You've removed my sin as far as the West is from the East.
Lord, Forgive Me for not believing You've forgiven me.

Lord, Forgive me for not believing You've forgiven me.
Lord, Forgive me for not believing You've forgiven me.
I was like a sinking ship, lost and tossed by an angry sea.
Lord, Forgive Me for not believing You've forgiven me.

The things I do, I shouldn't do, Lord, I know it's so.
The things I should do, why I don't, I don't know.
Who shall deliver me, Oh wretched man that I am.
Who would ever thought that I'd be bought
By the blood of the Lamb.

The man in the mirror I dreaded to see.
I met the enemy and he was me.

Then your love broke through, opened my blinded eyes to see
Lord, forgive me for not believing You've forgiven me.

He Just Wouldn't Listen

My heart's been broken by the burden of betraying
The only One Who ever loved me enough to die.
I know I'm so undeserving,
Each time I try to serve Him
I fall so far behind until I cry,
"Jesus, why would you even offer me the time of day?
You've got every reason to leave me here,
Go your own way.
I know I deserve your judgment Lord for being so untrue."
Then He smiles, says, "Come here Child,
No matter what you do.
You'll never keep me from loving you."

I even tried to talk him out of loving me
But He Just wouldn't listen.
He wouldn't pay me no mind.
I even tried to talk Him out of loving me.
He said, "Child, stop wasting our time."

Now, what do you do with a love like that?
"Lord, into your arms I fall."
Suffering love held nothing back.

WWMD What Would Mohammed Do?

Take this wretched soul, my God,
I surrender all.

Bob McLeod

Pillar Five: The Hajj, *the crowd gathers*

The fifth and final Pillar of Islam is the annual pilgrimage to Mecca in Saudi Arabia (Hajj). This is an obligation only for those who are physically and financially able to perform it. Nevertheless, about two million people go to Mecca each year from every corner of the globe. This provides a unique opportunity for those of different nations to meet one another. Although Mecca is always filled with visitors, the annual Hajj begins in the twelfth month of the Islamic year (which is lunar, not solar, so that Hajj and Ramadan fall sometimes in summer, sometimes in winter.) Pilgrims wear special clothes: simple garments which strip away distinctions of class and culture, as a reminder that all stand equal before God.

The rites of the Hajj, which are of Abrahamic origin, include circling the Kaba seven times, and going seven times between the mountains of Safa and Marwa, as did Hagar during her search for water. Then the pilgrims stand together on the wide plain of Arafa and join in prayers for God's forgiveness, in what is often thought of as a preview of the last judgment.

In previous centuries, the Hajj was an arduous undertaking. Today, however, Saudi Arabia provides millions of people with water, modern transport, and the most up-to-date health facilities.

A festival known as the "Eid al-Adha" marks the close of the Hajj. It is celebrated with prayers and the exchange of gifts in Muslim communities everywhere. This, and the "Eid al-Fitr"(a feast day commemorating the end of Ramadan) are the main festivals of the Muslim calendar.

In Bible-belt America we also have large religious gatherings. These gatherings are not considered a formal obligation however. They are sometimes called, "Camp Meetings" or "Festivals." Christian celebrities headline the events. The more famous they are, the more people will come. These festivals are often times preceded by massive marketing campaigns. Sometimes they even take place on a luxury cruise ship.

When large numbers of people gather for any reason there is a peculiar and even mystical energy. It's as if the crowd has one mind. There are those who are very skilled in manipulating the crowd, sometimes even behind the scenes. It's like leashing and leading a mindless beast that will gladly empty his pockets. The crowd, very often is deceived, giving a superficial but powerful sense of validity and authenticity to whoever is the headline.

We must not be deceived into believing that masses of people and masses of money validate truth. Crowds and opinions come and go like the waves of a shallow sea. If public opinion had any clout with God, then Barabbas would be Lord instead of Jesus.

Bob McLeod

Jackass
Numbers 22:30

The reverend stood tall.
The reverend stood proud.
Through the TV cameras and the wrap around sound
The preacher man preached real loud.
Many women would faint.
Many men would too.
They were deceived, probably never knew,
God'll speak through any Jackass that He chooses to.

So, don't praise me and I won't praise you.
Without Jesus we're sinners through and through.
Don't praise me and I won't praise you.
God'll speak through any Jackass that He chooses to.

No flesh will glory in His presence.
The prophet Balaam would certainly agree.
God'll speak through any Jackass that He chooses to.
My dear friend, that includes the likes of you and me.

Freedom

Bob McLeod

According to the Book

Webster's Thesaurus says that a sermon is a "long tedious speech, lecture, harangue, tirade; reproof, admonition, rebuke; dressing-down, tongue-lashing diatribe." Wonder where he got that? I didn't know Webster was born and raised in the Bible belt too!

When I hear the word "sermon," I think of an exhortation that has a dynamic influence upon a culture. We've always had our preachers, and it was their sermons that most influenced the people of their time.

We know it's a sermon when it's blasting out from under a steeple or the loudspeakers of a mosque. But the most effective, socially compelling sermons usually aren't recognized as such.

In America, unrecognizable preachers are constantly bombarding us from every direction with every imaginable admonition. Their sermons are being preached twenty-four hours a day, and there seems to be no escape.

We hear them in our songs and on radio and TV talk shows. We see them on bumper stickers, T-shirts, billboards, and even tattoos. They are sermons, that more often than not, promote a self-indulgent, vindictive and rebellious life style. The end result is always destruction and death. Just look around. It's obvious.

The most destructive sermons, however, are subtle and cloaked in the appearance of righteousness, benevolence and the healing of social ills.

Bob McLeod

What an incredibly gifted evangelist and preacher Adolph Hitler was! The Christian Church was his springboard into power! Christians, especially Baptists, loved him, prayed for him and praised God for sending him, that is until......

Beware the angel of light:

From the Bible:
Matthew 24:5,11
"For many will come in my name, claiming, 'I am the Christ, and will deceive many, and many false prophets will appear and deceive many people."

2 Corinthians 11:13,15,18
"For such men are false apostles, deceitful workmen, masquerading as apostles of Christ. And no wonder, for Satan himself masquerades as an angel of light. It is not surprising, then, if his servants masquerade as servants of righteousness. Their end will be what their actions deserve."

A person who is deceived doesn't know he's deceived or else he wouldn't be deceived. In the light of that simple truth, I can't help but wonder, "Am I the one who's really deceived?"

Either Jesus Christ is God and He's alive, or He's not. Could the Muslims be right? Is my Judeo-Christian ethnic upbringing wrong? Am I hopelessly trapped in my culture? What is truth anyway? Does anybody really know? So many different people are preaching so many different things, and they all seem so sincere and confident!

The one who believes that he's above deception is the one who is most deceived. He thinks he knows it all, even that which hasn't yet been discovered! Now that's deception!

How do I know if I'm being deceived? This can only be resolved by my being completely honest with myself and with my Maker. *I have to do one-on-one business with Him.*

But, in order to do one-on-one business with Him, I must first admit that I'm helpless without Him. *My independence must die!* I must face my helplessness. It's called *"humbling myself before God."*

The one great deception is, *"I don't need God! I am master of my fate and captain of my own soul. It's my life and I'll live it like I want to! Leave me alone! I can do it myself."* That's like stubbornly insisting that I can breathe without oxygen all the while slowly suffocating!

My Will Be Done

Your truth is ugly. My Truth is not.
Your truth says I'm going the wrong way
But I prefer the truth that I've got.
Your truth says, "Suffer."
My truth says, "Take your ease."
Your truth says "surrender."
I'd much rather do as I please.
Leave me alone. My Will Be Done.

Your truth is born in a manger.
Now how unimpressive can you be?
My truth boasts in our crowd of people,
High steeples and prophets with PhDs.
My truth loves to stand tall and proud for everyone to see
Your truth says I must humbly bow and fall to my knees.
Leave me alone. My Will Be Done.

The journey's over. My life is at its end.
Who's that just around the corner, a foe or a friend?
The darkness surrounds me. I don't want to die.
Reality has found me. I fell for the lie.
He leaves me alone and says to me for eternity,
Thy Will Be Done.

As soon as I heard Elvis sing the hit classic written by Paul Anka, *"I Did it My Way,"* I was ready to take on the world, my way! I felt invincible! I was determined and ready to march into hell for whatever I considered a heavenly cause! *My life!* My way! *Me and Elvis!*

Only trouble is, that fool-hearted philosophy doesn't work. It makes no provision for all the countless variables that are out of our control, including suffering and death. God only knows how many in the World Trade Center on September 11, 2001, were doing it *"my way."*

Elvis had it all, but he could not face life without the drugs that eventually killed him. By his own admission he was a miserable, tormented and lonely man, all the while doing it *"my way."* And our world today is full of miserable, tormented and lonely Elvis imitators!

How can I know that what I believe is true? The proof is always in the pudding. Is my life blessed or is it cursed? Never mind who or what I might think is to blame. Is life working for me? Am I being fulfilled? Does my sense of well-being depend on money? Can I enjoy being alone? Do I have assurance and peace that is not based on circumstances? Does bitterness and resentment torment me? Can I sleep at night? For the most part, do I enjoy being here? Do I live in fear? Am I imprisoned by guilt, regret and shame? When I consider that inevitable and necessary part of life called death, does it torment me? *Is what I believe working?* If not, then I may want to consider believing something else.

God spoke a Word of communication into the earth. *That Word of communication was Himself.* He spoke in a way that people from every tongue and nation could understand. The language He chose was "a physical demonstration!" *God Almighty became flesh and blood and publicly died a criminal's death on a cross!*

According to the Bible:

John 1: selected verses:
"In the beginning was the Word, and the Word was with God, and the Word was God. He was with God in the beginning.

Through him all things were made; without him nothing was made that has been made. In him was life, and that life was the light of men. The light shines in the darkness, but the darkness has not understood it.

He was in the world, and though the world was made through him, the world did not recognize him. He came to that which was his own, but his own did not receive him. Yet to all who did receive him, to those who believed in his name, he gave the right to become children of God—children born not of natural descent, not of human decision or a husband's will, but born of God.

The Word became flesh and made his dwelling among us. We have seen his glory, the glory of the One and only, who came from the Father, full of grace and truth".

He had to be born of a virgin!

Matthew 1:23
   "The virgin will be with child and will give birth to a son, and they will call him Emmanuel" —which means, "God with us."

He had to be without sin! (Self Indulgent Nature)

Hebrews 4:15
   "For we do not have a high priest who is unable to sympathize with our weaknesses, but we have one who has

been tempted in every way, just as we are—yet was without sin."

He took upon Himself the Divine judgment that every selfish thought and deed deserves and requires!

Romans 5: selected:
"You see, at just the right time, when we were still powerless, Christ died for the ungodly. Very rarely will anyone die for a righteous man, though for a good man someone might possibly dare to die. ***But God demonstrates his own love for us in this: While we were still sinners, Christ died for us.***

Since we have now been justified by his blood, how much more shall we be saved from God's wrath through him! For if, when we were God's enemies, we were reconciled to him through the death of his Son, how much more, having been reconciled, shall we be saved through his life!

Not only is this so, but we also rejoice in God through our Lord Jesus Christ, through whom we have now received reconciliation".

The Lord Jesus Christ took your place and mine at Calvary that day!

2 Corinthians 5:21
"God made him who had no sin to be sin for us, so that in him we might become the righteousness of God."

Bob McLeod

All of humanity has been forgiven and therefore made righteous. Those who receive Him (Jesus) experience life and life in abundance.

2 Corinthians 5:17,18,19:
"Therefore, if anyone is in Christ, he is a new creation; the old has gone, the new has come! All this is from God, who reconciled us to himself through Christ and gave us the ministry of reconciliation: that God was reconciling the world to himself in Christ, not counting men's sins against them."

John 10:10
"Jesus said, 'The thief comes only to steal and kill and destroy; I have come that they may have life, and have it more abundantly.'"

Those who are trying to *"do right to be right"* are rejecting God's sacrifice and forgiveness. They are deceived into believing that there is an acceptable *"do it yourself way to Heaven."*

The religions of men claim that there is good in every person and right they are. But there's also selfishness and bad in every person and that's what disqualifies one from God's perfect Heaven!

The curses do not come because of what we do or don't do. The curses come from rejecting the Lord Jesus Christ, His sacrifice, and His love!

WWMD What Would Mohammed Do?

Liar or Messiah

You ask me if I think you are going to hell
Just because you don't believe like I do.
Well, what I really think doesn't count for much at all.
All that really matters is the truth.
You say you think Jesus was a good and moral man,
A great teacher like Mohammed who died.
Well, Jesus had the nerve to say,
"He's the only way"
And a good and moral man wouldn't lie,

Jesus is a liar or else He's the Messiah.
And would a liar really lay down His life for a lie.
He came to earth and He passed through hell.
He was raised from the dead
To deliver us from an everlasting fire!
He's the Messiah.
He's the Messiah.

You will reject Him, or else you will receive Him.
You will deny Him, or else you will believe Him.
Do you dare to stake eternity
On half-hearted alibis?
Receive Him now, or else call Him a lie.

Bob McLeod

According to the Bible, Jesus Christ is alive right now!

Revelations 1:18
   "I am the Living One; I was dead, and behold I am alive forever and ever!"

The Debate
Proverbs 3:5-7

Someone asked me why I rely on the promises of Heaven
And how I can place my faith in someone who seems unseen.
The point they're out to make with an intellectual debate,
Is that salvation is a fool hearted dream.
Well when it's my turn to reply,
I look 'um right dead in the eye and say,
"OK friend, let's approach it from your point of view.
Your opinion ought to be respected. Let's put it all in perspective.
Sit back, relax, 'cause I got some good news for you."
There's just no way you're going to understand it.
That's just the way that He planned it.
The road to Heaven's not paved by a PHD degree.
You may have a brilliant mind, even rival Albert Einstein,
But don't let that cheat you out of being free.
Admit your need and let Him let you see.
So many have tried to doubt Him. So many have died without Him.

So many are lost and they struggle needlessly.
We all have the same need inside of us.
He offers His love in spite of us.
Let Him lift your burden, give you joy and everlasting peace.
Surrender to His power and then you won't be devoured
By the unseen forces that control you by your foolish pride.
Jesus died that we might live. Receive the love He longs to give,
And then, hallelujah you will see the light shining from the other side!
Become as a little child
The key is humility.

Since all of us are deceived in some way, how can I be 100% right with less than 100% of the light? We need someone to guide us out of our deception, and that someone is our Shepherd, the Lord Jesus Christ.

As we WWJD, "Walk With Jesus Daily," He will then lead us out of our deception. The Book calls it, *"walking in the Light."*

Psalm 89:14,15,16
"Righteousness and justice are the foundation of your throne; love and faithfulness go before you. Blessed are those who have learned to acclaim you, **who walk in the light of your presence, O LORD.** *They rejoice in your name all day long; they exult in your righteousness".*

Bob McLeod

1 John 1:7

"But if we walk in the light, as he is in the light, *we have fellowship with one another, and the blood of Jesus, his Son, purifies us from all sin."*

Here's what happens to those who refuse God's Light and walk in their own:

From the Book:
Isaiah 50:11
"But now, all you who light fires and provide yourselves with flaming torches, ***go, walk in the light of your fires and of the torches you have set ablaze.*** *This is what you shall receive from my hand:* ***You will lie down in torment."***

Reality Road
John 14:2

I use to live on Memory Lane,
In a house called Guilt, Regret and Shame.
Struggling with the past I couldn't change,
Pining my life away on Memory Lane.
So I moved to another House on Memory Lane,
The House of Glory faded just as fast as it came.
Longing for loved ones gone, hopeless and vain,
In the House of Faded Glory on Memory Lane.
So I moved out of there to a place not so far,

WWMD What Would Mohammed Do?

The street sign said, "Anticipation Boulevard."
Anxiety's House, I couldn't even get out of bed.
Paralyzed by fear, worry and dread.
So I moved to the inner city. It's a pity but it's true.
Fussin' and fightin' all day and all night down on Anger Avenue.
The turmoil and strife nearly cost me my life.
The same will happen to you, living down on Anger Avenue.

Then I heard someone knockin' at the door.
He said, "The whole neighborhood's on fire.
Man, you don't want to hang around here no more!
He said, "Follow Me." I said, "Okay, where we gonna go?"
He said, "To my Father's House on Reality Road."

Reality Road, that's where you want to be.
You can know the Truth. The Truth will set you free.
Free from the past. Free from tomorrow too.
On Reality Road there's a mansion for you!

Bob McLeod

Satan, the Adversary is Necessary

Satan, or the devil, according to the Bible and the Quran is a rebellious angel expelled from Heaven by God. He's at the heart of every act of evil in the world and has become a common scapegoat in the mind of many religious people. Whenever something we consider bad happens we can always blame Satan. Whenever someone opposes or challenges the doctrines of our religious club, we can all agree that they're *"of the devil."*

Ellen G. White, the founder of the Seventh day Adventists, wrote a book named, *"The Great Controversy."* There are many other books in our religious history that say basically the same thing: "A Good God has a controversy with a bad devil."

Many Muslims reject Christians for rejecting Mohammed; therefore Christians are considered to be of Satan. Many Christians claim Muslims are of Satan because they reject Christ.

"God's on our side and you're on the devil's side. How do I know? My religious leader's interpretation of our Holy Book tells me so!"

Did you dare to *yawn* while reading this book? Shame on you!

WWMD What Would Mohammed Do?

From the Holy Book, *Hadith—Bukhari 4:509*,
Narrated Abu Huraira

The Prophet said, *"Yawning is from Satan and if anyone of you yawns, he should check his yawning as much as possible, for if anyone of you (during the act of yawning) should say: 'Ha', Satan will laugh at him."*

A "Fatwa" is a legal statement in Islam issued by a "Mufti" (a religious lawyer) concerning a specific issue. Here's a Fatwa issued February 28, 1998:

"We—with Allah's help—call on every Muslim who believes in Allah, and wishes to be rewarded, to comply with Allah's order to kill the Americans and plunder their money wherever and whenever they find it. We also call on Muslim ulema, leaders, youths, and soldiers to launch the raid on Satan's U.S. troops and the devil's supporters allying with them, and to displace those who are behind them so that they may learn a lesson."

Signed: Osama Bin Laden and other holy men whose names I can't spell.

Iranian Muslim leader Ayatollah Khomeini was Time Magazines "Man of the Year" in 1979. In 1989, he and his Iranian colleagues found novelist Salmon Rushdie's book, "The Satanic Verses", offensive. They signed a fatwa against him, calling for his death and offering more than two million dollars for his murder. Rushdie wasn't in any "rush to die", so he went into hiding. Three Iranian officials suspected of attempting to organize his murder were expelled from Britain the following year. In Tehran, the

Iranian parliament, the Majlis, reviewed the execution order and refused to rescind it.

Satan is real. The Bible refers to him as an adversary *(1 Peter 5:8)* and a liar *(John 8:44)*, but using him as a scapegoat only gives credibility to his lies and further intensifies the bondage and torment.

Overcoming Adversity

Richmond Flowers was a lightning fast superstar and Olympic hurdler from prestigious Sidney Lanier High School in Montgomery, Alabama. I was a flat-footed, country boy, stump jumper from Osh Gosh, a little community just between Jacksonville and Hokes Bluff, right near Possum Trot Road in NE Alabama.

It was the Alabama State High School Track meet, 1965. High School athletes from all over the state had converged upon Montgomery for this highly touted event.

It was the first heat: 120-yard high hurdles. Even though I was terrified, I tried to appear confident as I stooped down in the starting blocks, extending and shaking each leg behind me. I'd never extended and shaken my legs like that before, but that's the way Richmond was doing it and he was in the lane next to me.

My high school buddies were in the stands cheering for me, absolutely amazed and amused that I would be running against the famous Richmond Flowers!

The crowd came to its feet and, despite my self-conscious feelings of intimidation and embarrassment; I remained neck-and-neck with Richmond Flowers! That is, until they shot that gun! He sailed over the last hurdle and crossed the finish line as I skinned my knee knocking over the second hurdle! I know what it is to be left in the dust!

I didn't win any medals that day, but I began to learn a wonderful lesson about life and about the certain adversities that we all face.

Richmond Flowers was physically equipped and prepared for the race. He saw the hurdles (obstacles) as opportunities. I was neither physically equipped nor prepared. The hurdles (obstacles) to me were problems. Richmond was confident and secure. I was fearful and insecure.

How can I view life's obstacles as opportunities rather than problems? How can I face adversity confidently rather than fearfully? How do I become equipped? How can I be prepared? How can I be victorious in the race of life, the race that really counts? How can I overcome?

First, I must recognize the absolute sovereignty of our Creator. He has all power and authority in Heaven and Earth! *Matthew 28:18*

Second, I must recognize His unfailing, untiring and merciful love for me.

Third, I must recognize that the life extends far beyond the confines of time and space and the sovereign Creator's purpose for humanity is eternal, not temporal. The temporal is preparation for the eternal.

As I recognize the Creator's sovereignty, unfailing love for me, and eternal purpose, I then will realize that the adversary is necessary. Adversity is a refining tool in the Potter's hand used to shape, mold, purify and prepare us for eternity. The devil, our adversary, is a vital factor in God's redemptive equation.

Here are some verses from the Book that haunted me for years. "Why are these in the Bible?" I wondered. "Sure doesn't sound like a loving God to me?"

Proverbs 16:4

The Lord hath made all things for himself: yea, even the wicked for the day of evil.

Isaiah 54:16

Behold, I have created the smith that bloweth the coals in the fire, and that bringeth forth an instrument for his work; and I have created the destroyer to destroy.

Amos 3:6

Shall a trumpet be blown in the city, and the people not be afraid? Shall there be evil in a city, and the Lord hath not done it?

Matthew 10:28

And fear not them which kill the body, but are not able to kill the soul: but rather fear him which is able to destroy both soul and body in hell.

WWMD What Would Mohammed Do?

How can a loving God be in control of evil? Before we can understand, we must humble ourselves and resist every temptation to sit in judgment of Him!

Romans 9:20-23

But who are you, O man, to talk back to God? Shall what is formed say to him who formed it, 'Why did you make me like this?' Does not the potter have the right to make out of the same lump of clay some pottery for noble purposes and some for common use? What if God, choosing to show his wrath and make his power known, bore with great patience the objects of his wrath—prepared for destruction?

When I stop defining how I think God ought to be, and humbly accept Him as He chooses to reveal Himself, then I will began to see.

Just because our Creator is in control of evil, that does not mean He is responsible for it! Evil is the result of our rebellion against Him. How can He be responsible for that? He's the One rebelled against!

When we consider the cross of our Lord Jesus Christ, we can never, ever question the mercy, goodness and love of God! He suffered the full impact and consequence of our selfish rebellion in order that the world through Him might be saved!

Adversity, sin, evil and hatred gave God the opportunity to demonstrate His unfailing, unconditional love! And so it continues today: darkness providing the opportunity for Light!

The adversary is necessary for three primary reasons:

1) Drives us to **PRAYER**!

Prayer is communion with God. Grace is His unmerited favor, which empowers us and produces a heart capable of obedience to Him. According to *James 4:6 "God opposes the proud but gives grace to the humble."* Therefore, humiliation is an expression of His love. It gets us in a position to receive grace! An old country song of years ago said it well: "Pride's not hard to swallow once you've chewed it long enough."

Many a self sufficient, tough guy pretender has been brought to his knees by adversity, and it's on our knees that we meet God and discover the grace to be one with Him!

2) For PREPARATION.

You and I were born with the *Genesis 3:10* selfish nature of the first Adam. Selfishness is high treason against God and is not allowed in Heaven *(Isaiah 14:12-15)*. Jesus Christ, the last Adam, Who is our example *(1 Peter 2:21)*, is selfless *(1 John 3:16)!* We are being transformed from selfishness to selflessness and it's being accomplished through our submission and surrender to Him. Adversity and suffering provide the crucible where this decentralizing takes place.

1 John 3:2

Dear friends, now we are children of God, and what we will be has not yet been made known. But we know that when *he appears, <u>we shall be like him</u> (selfless), for we shall see him as he is.*

A number of times over the years people have asked me to pray with them and ask God to make the devil leave them alone. That would totally defeat life's purpose! It would be like Richmond Flowers asking his coach before practice to remove the hurdles!

Revelation 3:21:
"To him that overcometh will I grant to sit with me in my throne, even as I also overcame, and am set down with my Father in his throne."

A hurdler can't be a hurdler without hurdles and an overcomer can't be an overcomer without adversity!
Here's a key overcoming verse from the Bible:

Revelation 12:11:
And they overcame him by the blood of the Lamb, and by the word of their testimony; and they loved not their lives unto the death. (Selflessness again!)

As you give your life to Him He then will carry you over every obstacle! Remember, without Him, we can do nothing! *(John 15:5)*

The Adversary is also necessary:

3) For **PROPULSION**!

Satan's attack is always God's opportunity! Every Calvary has a resurrection! What the devil means for harm, God means for good! Every time Satan swings, he hits himself! The tares fertilize the wheat. The same flood that destroyed all but Noah and his family lifted the ark!

History (<u>His story</u>) is one example after another. The holocaust birthed the Nation Israel; Watergate birthed Prison Fellowship, etc.!

This verse from the Bible says it all:

2 Corinthians 4:17-18 (Amplified):
For our light, momentary affliction (this slight distress of the passing hour) is ever more and more abundantly preparing and producing and achieving for us an everlasting weight of glory (beyond all measure, excessively surpassing all comparisons and all calculations, a vast and transcendent glory and blessedness never to cease!

Adversity reveals our helplessness. In our revealed helplessness, we cry out to Him and when we cry out to Him, we find Him always and forever faithful!

This is how our confidence in Him grows. Our confidence in Him is our faith, our overcoming faith! Faith that is the *"evidence of things not seen!" (Hebrews 11:1).*

WWMD What Would Mohammed Do?

We must also be careful to avoid imaginary hurdles! Don't fight battles you're not in. There's no grace for it.

E.L. Green's Store
Matthew 6:25-34

One night I dreamed I lost my lady after I lost my job.
Gettin' scared to death of dyin' but
Life's gettin rougher than a corncob.
This keepin' pace in the rat race will get a body further behind.
Anxiety's closin' in on me and giving me a worried mind.
Decided I'd take a drive to the country. Sure beats pacin' the floor.
Wound up in a back wood place called E.L. Green's Store.
There's an ole' man sittin' out front on a bench,
Weathered brow and a toothless smile.
He said, "Have a seat, Son, you look beat."
Then he told me somethin' that made my trip worthwhile.
He said: "Most folks are fightin' battles that they ain't even in.
I don't know how they ever expect to win.
See that there dog a chasin' his tail?
Don't laugh, he's just actin' like most men.
And most folks are fightin' battles they ain't even in."
He said, "Why worry about tomorrow, son when all ya got is today?
It's gonna all work out in the end,

Bob McLeod

That is, for them who'll trust and pray.
We'll never leave this here world alive, boy
But this world ain't all that there is. Why don't you let Jesus love you?
He'll fight your battles 'fer ya and make ya one of His!"
At that moment I begin to feel a peace within.
I fell in love with Love Himself and He became my Friend.
I headed back home but not alone. I got a new outlook on life.
And I ain't worried anymore since I gave up the fight.

Horatio G. Spafford was hit hard by adversity. A forty-three-year old Chicago businessman, he suffered financial disaster in the Great Chicago Fire of 1871. He and his wife were still grieving over the death of their son shortly before the fire, and he realized they needed to get away for a vacation. Knowing that their friend Dwight L. Moody was going to be preaching in evangelistic campaigns in England that fall, Spafford decided to take the entire family to England. His wife and four daughters went ahead on the liner, SS Ville du Havre, and he planned to follow in a few days.

But on the Atlantic Ocean, the ship was struck by an iron sailing vessel and sank within twelve minutes. Two hundred twenty-six lives were lost—including the Spaffords' four daughters. When the survivors were brought to shore at Cardiff, Wales, Mrs. Spafford cabled her husband, "Saved alone."

Spafford booked passage on the next ship. As they were crossing the Atlantic, the captain pointed out the place where he thought the SS Ville du Havre had gone down. That night, Spafford penned the famous hymn that continues to minister comfort to millions:

"...When sorrows like sea billows roll; whatever my lot, Thou hast taught me to say, even so, it is well, It Is Well with my soul... though Satan should buffet, tho' trials should come, let this blest assurance control, That Christ has regarded my helpless estate and hath shed His own blood for my soul..."

Romans 5:2-4

Through whom we have gained access by faith into this grace in which we now stand. And we rejoice in the hope of the glory of God. Not only so, but we also rejoice in our sufferings, because we know that suffering produces perseverance; perseverance, character; and character, hope.

Hebrews 12:1

Therefore, since we are surrounded by such a great cloud of witnesses, let us throw off everything that hinders, and the sin that so easily entangles, and let us run with perseverance the race marked out for us.

1 John 5:4

For whatsoever is born of God overcometh the world: and this is the victory that overcometh the world, even our faith.

Bob McLeod

May you and I honor our Lord by faith, seeing adversity as our "opportunity" rather than our "problem"; knowing, indeed, that God is causing "all things to work together for our good because we love Him and are called according to His purpose!" *(Romans 8:28)*

Birth Pangs

There are many in Muslim and Christian Communities who are consumed with a political agenda.

From The Book:
Proverbs 17:24
Wisdom is before him that hath understanding; but the eyes of a fool are in the ends of the earth.

To have a mindset that entertains only "time/space" earth issues is to face a personal disintegration with no hope. We are all physically disintegrating. Suffering and death has a way of spoiling every party. Wars, disasters, and pestilence don't increase the death rate. The death rate is one per person.

Have you ever spent a successful evening playing Monopoly with some friends? What a respected and enviable winner you were! You owned hotels, banks, houses, and there was a large stack of money right in front of you for all to see.

You certainly could have qualified for mayor, governor or president had that been part of the game. And then, everyone became tired. They said, "good night" and left you to put all the pieces back in the box! Your success had no lasting significance and so it is with all the passing kingdoms of men. One day all of the stuff goes back in the box!

Bob McLeod

So What

You say you've some money; You'll never work again.
You make the maidens marvel.
Got a bunch of big-shot friends.
So What, So What?
You say that you've got power. You say you've got prestige.
You're chairman of the board and you do just what you please.
So What? So What?

So What have you got that won't rot in just a few days?
So What have you got that will last beyond the grave?
So What, So What have you got?

You say you've got a jet plane, a limo for a car.
You've found your claim to fame.
You run around with movie stars.
So What? So What?

You say you made the cover of People Magazine.
You've got yourself a bodyguard who's ugly, big and mean!
So What? So What?
If you refuse Jesus Christ
How will you find eternal life?
So What? So What have you got?

WWMD What Would Mohammed Do?

The Child

'Tis the *"Night Before Christmas"* in a crude cattle stall. The young and innocent Mary never knew it would be this painful. She's about to become *"Mother Mary."*

She feels so helpless. There's nowhere she can go. There's no way she can escape what, so far, is the most horrible, excruciating ordeal of her life. She feels like a trapped animal, a prisoner in her own skin.

The pain engulfs her like the pulsating waves of an angry, violent, storm-tossed sea. The brief moments of relief between the contractions are becoming less and less frequent.

She's lost all dignity. She's lost all control. She screams! She moans. She gasps for breath. She screams again! Will it ever end?

Those around her scream also, *"This is a senseless tragedy!* It ought not to be! She can't take it any more! Somebody do something! Don't just sit there! Can't you see the horror? Can't you hear the screams? Doesn't anyone care? How long are you going to let this go on?"

Childbirth, the storm before the calm: a mother's body being pulled inside out! Torture! Torment! Suffering! Agony!

Outside the stable there's a group of innocent "by standers." Hearing the repeated screams of agony coming from the stable, they forsake all innocence and refuse to "stand by" any longer! They get involved! Reacting to what at first appears to be a call to heroism, they burst through the entrance to the stable and race toward the screaming "mother to be." Mary's husband, Joseph is manhandled and violently pushed out of the way!

"This is an abomination," one shouts! "God's going to hold us responsible for this!" another keeps shouting.

"All it takes for evil to prevail is for good men to do nothing!" seems to be another favorite slogan. The well-meaning zealots' anger increases with every cry of the mother's travail.

They pray. They march. They sing hymns. They recruit. They raise money for their cause. They complain. They blame. They accuse. They make signs and march around the stable angrily condemning those who don't get involved with them.

A fight breaks out! A midwife who is assisting in the delivery is suddenly shoved out of the way! The angry mob of self-proclaimed medical experts surrounds the "mother to be" and frantically fight to stop the pain! Their only concern is "stopping the pain." To some it appears noble, even heroic and responsible, but their minds and emotions are obsessed with *"WHAT IS"* without any consideration of *"WHAT IS TO COME."*

Totally oblivious to the reality of a child being born, they are determined to take matters into their own hands and do whatever it takes to stop the pain.

Their sleeves are rolled up. Their faces are set like flint. Their cause has become their God.

"Praise Jehovah! We are making a difference!" one zealot shouts as he detects a brief period of momentary relief between the birth pangs. Then, another contraction! "What's going on?" "We must work harder! We must get more 'God fearing' people involved! We've got to 'wake up the church! We've got to stop this pain or God will judge us all!"

The group continues to scramble and scream—expending all their energy and resources in total futility, refusing to let go of their false hope, and refusing to submit to the sovereign, natural process of a child being born—and not just any child. *This child is the Christ.*

We are living in an age of unprecedented social, political, economic and ecological turmoil and travail. It's not possible here to itemize, in detail, all of the atrocities or describe the continuous, intensifying anguish and pain that haunts and stalks every one of us. Our families, communities and governments are all at risk. For a detailed, grotesque, blow-by-blow account, just simply tune in to CNN Headline News anytime, night or day.

No one is immune to the intensified suffering of this hour. There's rampant self-destruction, child abuse, murder, rape, arson, sexual atrocities, drug and alcohol addiction, bio-terrorism, pestilence, famines, and every form of natural disaster, including fires, floods, earthquakes, tornadoes, tidal waves and hurricanes. Deadly pollution, escalating and intensified violence, hatred, hypocrisy, exploitation and every manner of deviation and destruction has become the norm.

Bob McLeod

Many well-meaning Christians have taken on the cause of social change, with their minds and emotions set on *"WHAT IS"* without any consideration of *"WHAT IS TO COME."*

People are terribly frustrated, distressed, angry, and blaming each other, simply because what Jesus said would happen, is happening.

Listen to His words from the Bible:

Matthew 24:4,6-8:
"See to it that no one misleads you... and you will be hearing of wars and rumors of wars; see that you are not frightened, for those things MUST TAKE PLACE, but that is not yet the end. For nation will rise against nation, (The word translated "nation" here is "ethnos," from which we get our word, "ethnic." Racial tension is a fulfillment of this prophecy) *and kingdom against kingdom, and in various places there will be famines and earthquakes."*

These things we perceive to be and refer to as "senseless" aren't "senseless" at all. Jesus goes on to tell us the "sense" in them:

"But all these things are merely the beginning of BIRTH PANGS!"

Someone is being born! The intimate, eternal Bride of the Lord Jesus Christ has been conceived within the womb of Mother Earth and is being born! *"WHAT IS"* is birth pangs. *"WHAT IS TO COME"* is the fulfilled purpose of God's creation, a glorious marriage union, the intimate consummation of eternal love and everlasting ecstasy!

Revelation 19:7:
"Let us rejoice and be glad and give Glory to Him, for the marriage of the Lamb has come and His Bride has made herself ready!"

The only hope (but what a hope it is!) is to see things from God's eternal perspective.

Our life within this tiny, fleeing, time/space box called Planet Earth is not all that there is! We are on our way to GLORY and God Almighty is causing everything to serve His ultimate eternal purpose!

Ephesians 1:11:
"Also, we have obtained an inheritance, having been predestined according to His purpose who works ALL THINGS after the counsel of His will."

In the preceding vision, Mother Mary is a type of Mother Earth. Her anguish and birth pangs represent the suffering and travail we're experiencing today. The zealots who are trying to stop the birth pangs are the well meaning, but improperly-focused, political activists, who are reacting to the pain, focusing on *"WHAT IS"* with no consideration of *"WHAT IS TO COME."* The Baby being born, Who in the vision is Christ, is a type of His Bride (the true church) who is being formed and made into His very likeness, which is the selfless expression of God's Love.

With this in view, consider again these following verses from the Book:

2 Corinthians 4:17,18:

"For momentary, light affliction (WHAT IS) is producing for us an eternal weight of glory far beyond all comparison (WHAT IS TO COME)."

Hebrews 12:2:

"Fixing our eyes on Jesus, the Author and Perfecter of faith, Who for the joy set before Him (WHAT IS TO COME) endured the cross, despising the shame (WHAT IS), and has sat down at the right hand of the throne of God. For consider Him Who has endured such hostility by sinners against Himself, so that you may not grow weary and lose heart."

I John 3:2:

"Beloved, now we are children of God (WHAT IS), and it has not appeared as yet what we shall be. We know that, when He appears, we shall be like Him (WHAT IS TO COME), because we shall see Him just like He is."

Psalm 37 (Selected verses):

"Do not fret because of evil doers... for they will wither quickly like the grass and fade like the green herb. Trust in the Lord and do good; dwell in the land and cultivate faithfulness. Delight yourself in the Lord and He will give you the desires of your heart. Commit your way to the Lord, trust also in Him, and He will do it. He will bring forth your righteousness as the light, and your judgment as the noonday.

Rest in the Lord and wait patiently for Him... cease from anger and forsake wrath; do not fret, it leads only to evil doing. For evil doers will be cut off."

Matthew 16:23:
"...and Peter took Him aside and began to rebuke Him, saying, 'God forbid it, Lord! This shall never happen to you. But He turned and said to Peter, 'Get behind Me, Satan! You are a stumbling block to Me; for you are not setting your mind on God's interests (WHAT IS TO COME), but man's (WHAT IS)."

This is not to imply that all Christian political involvement is wrong or futile. Those who love the Lord are salt and light. *Salt is that which restrains evil and light is the visible Beacon of Hope.*

If our motive is to make this world a better place with our minds focused on the things of men *(WHAT IS)*, then we will be vulnerable to hopeless torment, deceived, and even used as an accomplice to the very evil, that we abhor.

If our motive is to please our Heavenly Father with our minds focused on Him and His eternal purpose *(WHAT IS TO COME)*, then we will be witnesses of His Kingdom that is not of this world *(John 18:36)*. We will be messengers of mercy and hope to this dying world. This is how salt and light are released.

Colossians 3:2
"*Set your mind on things above, not on things on the Earth.*"

The greatest tragedy that can befall a human being is to be at home in this earth.

2 Corinthians 5:6
"*...while we are at home in the body we are absent from the Lord.*"

John 16:33:
"*In this world we have trouble, but we can be of good cheer*"

Because... we are in the natural process of a child being born; and not just any child. This child is the Bride of Christ!

Matthew 24:35:
"*Heaven and earth will pass away, but My Words will by no means pass away...*"
"*Those with ears to hear, let them hear...*"

WWMD What Would Mohammed Do?

Billy and Bubba
(Romans 8:22,23)

*Billy and Bubba, twins in their mother's womb.
Billy and Bubba, 9 months sharing the same play room.
Snug and warm, safe from harm.
You might say, "Everything was cool."
Laughin' and splashin' in their own indoor swimming pool.
Then all at once they heard a groan and they felt a pain.
Billy said, "Bubba, don't leave me alone.
Life without you just won't be the same."
Bubba said, "Billy, I'm about to die."
Billy said, "Bubba, I'm about to cry."
Life is not at all what we expected.
Life is just a matter of perspective.
No need to reason why. Fear not my child,
Don't you know we never die?
What's your perspective?
Billy and Bubba, same room in the nursing home.
Billy and Bubba, 90 years have come and gone.
Blankets to keep them warm; no cause for alarm.
They were washed in the blood one day.
No fear of tomorrow. No fear of today.
Then Billy heard a groan and Bubba felt a pain.
Billy said, ""Bubba we're never alone.
Thank God, the Savior came!"
Bubba said, "Billy I'm about to die."
Billy said, "Bubba, I'll See you on the other side!"*

Bob McLeod

Self-Paralysis

From The Book:
Genesis 3:8-11
"Then the man and his wife heard the sound of the Lord God as he was walking in the garden in the cool of the day, and they hid from the Lord God among the trees of the garden. But the Lord God called to the man, 'Where are you?' He answered, 'I heard you in the garden, and I was afraid because I was naked; so I hid.' And he said, 'who told you that you were naked? Have you eaten from the tree that I commanded you not to eat from?'"

From The Noble Quran Al-A'raf 7:22
"So he (Satan) misled them (Adam and Eve) with deception. Then when they tasted of the tree, that which was hidden from them of their shame (private parts) became manifest to them and they began to stick together the leaves of Paradise over themselves (in order to cover their shame). And their Lord called out to them (saying): 'did I not forbid you that tree and tell you: Verily, Shaitân (Satan) is an open enemy unto you?'"

We've known Dale since he was a young boy. We watched him grow up. He was a best friend to our youngest son and was in and out of our home almost constantly. Dale was eighteen when his Dad died of cancer. Later, Dale found his

Dad's pain medication and it seemed to help him cope with the pain of his loss.

But the inevitable happened. The drugs betrayed him. His pain became intensified as the drugs infected his body and soul, choking the very life out of him.

Dale became an addict and, by the time he was twenty-five, his life had become totally unmanageable. He couldn't hold down a job and he was in and out of jail.

June 2000, Dale was court ordered to "Our Father's Arms," a Christian residential ministry in NE Alabama. He lived there with us for about two months and then moved out to be with his wife and newborn son.

We hoped he would continue to stay clean and have a productive life, but he didn't. On the night of June 30, 2001, Dale went to visit one of his so-called friends who offered him some drugs. After taking the drugs, Dale collapsed and lay unconscious for several hours before they took him to the emergency room of the local hospital. The prognosis was very bleak. "There's no brain activity. If he lives, he'll be a vegetable." the doctors said.

We went to see Dale right away. He was laying unconscious in the Intensive Care Unit. While we were there alone with him, we asked Jesus for a miracle. We prayed that Dale would be restored and that the remainder of his life would glorify God.

For a number of weeks the opposite seemed to happen. He had periodic seizures. He had chewed his tongue until it had become like ground beef, swollen, cut and bleeding. For this reason they had to place a plastic apparatus in his mouth. He also had to have a feeding tube, and his body had become so emaciated and disfigured that it became too disheartening and depressing for some to even go see him. It appeared that the doctors were right and Dale's life would be a tragic nightmare.

Several weeks later Dale was moved from ICU to a room in the Psychiatric Ward. I went there to visit him. When I entered the room I was surprised to see his eyes were open, his mouth was clear, and there was no longer a feeding tube down his throat. He was staring straight ahead with no expression. His entire body was obviously paralyzed. I knelt by his bed and looked into his eyes.

I talked to Dale as if he could understand me. I began sharing *Words from The Book* with him, emphasizing the cross:

"Dale, Jesus is the One Who created you, the One Who knows your every thought. He's with you now Dale and He loves you with a passionate, unfailing love. He's not mad at you. He's not ashamed of you. He shed His precious blood that day at Calvary in order for you to be forgiven. He's here to help you Dale. It's very important that you forgive everyone, Dale, including yourself! Jesus will help you. Receive His love, and let Him remove your guilt, your regret and your shame. Your relationship with Him is all that matters, Dale."

At that moment Dale began to weep uncontrollably, and I realized that he had understood exactly what I was saying. I began trying to establish two-way communication by asking him to blink his eyes in response to some questions. At first he did respond, but suddenly his eyes would become fixed with an unblinking stare. It became obvious that, the harder Dale tried to communicate, the less he was able. He was totally incapacitated by self-consciousness and fear.

I began sharing God's antidote for fear with him:

From The Bible:
1 John 4:18
"There is no fear in love. But perfect love drives out fear, because fear has to do with punishment."

Dale was released several weeks later and returned home and, as of this writing, continues to improve.

Dale's journey, his self-destruction and his on-going recovery, is an incredible object lesson for us. As we look at Dale, we can learn more about ourselves and come to a greater awareness of our own personal deliverance and healing.

What is self-consciousness? It's the S.I.N. nature. (**Self Indulgent Nature**) and we were all born with it.

Romans 3:23
"For all have sinned, and come short of the glory of God."

It's the "I, me, my, lie." I'm deceived into thinking that I'm the center of the Universe: *like the rooster who thought the sun came up just to hear him crow!*

What is the underlying cause of S.I.N. and self-consciousness? Quiet simply, it's rejection. The deepest human need is the need to be accepted (loved). Therefore, the deepest pain is the pain of rejection (hate). Each of us, without exception, gravitates toward acceptance and we flee from rejection.

God created us for Himself, to be recipients and communicators of His acceptance, which is His love. When our ancestors, Adam and Eve, chose to reject Him by disobeying His Word, they rejected love, acceptance and life. As a consequence, their progeny are born with a hollow emptiness: an insatiable, desperate and unsatisfied need. Most people live out their earthly lives looking for love in all the wrong places, slaves of self-consciousness.

Again from The Book:
Genesis 3:9,10:
"But the LORD God called to the man, 'Where are you?' He answered, 'I heard you in the garden, and I was afraid because I was naked; so I hid.' And God said, 'who told you that you were naked? Have you eaten from the tree that I commanded you not to eat from?'"

Many people are frantically driven to over-achieve; some try to feel important by identifying with an over-achiever, while others give up entirely, becoming so totally self-consumed, they have no direction and no consideration of anyone else.

Many if not most, highly successful, high profile people are miserable and restless. It's always the result of a fractured self-image brought on by rejection.

The only reason I would be driven to be "a somebody" is because deep inside I feel like I'm a nobody. Totally focused on me, I'm determined to prove myself. I long, and even lust, for the approval of men.

And if I achieve all that my heart longs for: success, acclaim, and money, what then? Will I finally be fulfilled? Barbara Walters asked Ted Turner what success meant to him; He cynically replied without hesitation, "It's an empty bag!"

The inevitable and ultimate consequence of S.I.N. caused by rejection is self-inflicted death.

Romans 6:23a
"For the wages of sin is death."

Fear, anxiety, depression, anger, offense, irritability, frustration, disappointment, strife, immorality, various addictions, and all the other negative expressions of human life are all indicators that S.I.N. is at work.

"I don't have a problem like that drug addict," you might say. "I'd never do illegal drugs, nor associate with anyone who does. I'm more respectable than that!"

You may be, but where do you turn for solace when you're disappointed and when you feel forsaken and rejected? It may not be your dad dying when you think you need him most. It may be a divorce, an unfaithful spouse, a business deal gone bad, or any number of things that cause you to question your self-worth.

Where do you turn? Is food your self-destructive weapon? Are you digging a grave with your teeth? Your tongue may not be chewed and bleeding, but what about the lining of your stomach? Perhaps your self-destructive compulsion is to avoid food. Anorexia Nervosa is epidemic.

Is alcohol killing you? Is it tobacco? Is it an obsession with your work or what you think other people think of you? You may be an adrenaline-junkie. That may be why violent and dangerous sports appeal to you so much. Perhaps it's pornography or sexual perversion. Often, even religion can be the breeding ground for offense, anger, disappointment and fear *(of men and/or of the devil.)*

We see rampant self-destruction not only in individuals, but society at large. Our bodies give us painful warning signals that our lifestyle is destructive, and what do our doctors do? They prescribe medication to help us ignore the warning signals as we defiantly continue on S.I.N.'s path of death and destruction.

Why do human beings have to have governments? Why do we need laws, judges, law enforcement agencies, jails, prisons, security systems and locks on our doors? It's all an effort to restrain the self-destructive S.I.N. nature of man.

We can also see this destruction working through our interpersonal relationships. Modern psychology calls it *"co-dependence."* It's when people are addicted to each other, one being the controller, the other, compliant. It can be the hen-pecked husband or the abused wife who refuses to leave. It can also be a controlling, dominating religious leader in a mosque or church.

Drug addicts and alcoholics always have a co-dependant someone enabling them. It may even be the Government through a disability check.

How can we be saved from ourselves? In the Book, *1 Corinthians 10:6*, we read, *"The things which happened to Israel happened as examples to us."* With this in mind, we can look at *Numbers 21:4-9* and learn a very valuable lesson:

4) *"They traveled from Mount Hor along the route to the Red Sea, to go around Edom. But the people grew impatient on the way;"* **Things weren't going their way (self-centered).**

5) *"They spoke against God and against Moses, and said, 'Why have you brought us up out of Egypt to die in the desert? There is no bread! There is no water! And we detest this miserable food!'"* **Complaining! Here are the symptoms of S.I.N at work.**

6) *"Then the LORD sent venomous snakes among them; they bit the people and many Israelites died."* **God doesn't like ungrateful, self-centered grumbling and complaining!**

7) *"The people came to Moses and said, 'we sinned when we spoke against the LORD and against you. Pray that the LORD will take the snakes away from us.' So Moses prayed for the people."* **Anything for self-preservation.**

Bob McLeod

8) *"The LORD said to Moses, 'Make a snake and put it up on a pole; anyone who is bitten can look at it and live."* **God provides mercy for self-centered people.**

9) *"So Moses made a bronze snake and put it up on a pole. Then when anyone was bitten by a snake and looked (Amplified: attentively, expectantly, with a steady and absorbing gaze) at the bronze snake, he lived."* **They had to look away from themselves to gaze upon the snake. This is a type of the Lord Jesus Christ being lifted up upon a cross. Here are His words to Nicodemus many years later:**

The Bible:
(John 3:14-17)
Just as Moses lifted up the snake in the desert, so the Son of Man must be lifted up, that everyone who believes in him may have eternal life. For God so loved the world that he gave his one and only Son, that whoever believes in him shall not perish but have eternal life. For God did not send his Son into the world to condemn the world, but to save the world through him."

Looking away from ourselves and fixing our attention upon the Lord Jesus Christ is where we find our healing!

Isaiah 45:22

"Look unto Me and be saved all ye ends of the earth. I am God and there is no other!"

Some counselors today *(even professing Christians)* are trained to analyze the snakes. It only adds to the confusion. When there's no repentance from selfishness to Christ, the only alternative is medication: sedate them as they continue to live in their self-induced hell.

Watchman Nee, a Chinese writer, teacher and church planter, who spent almost a third of his life imprisoned and tortured for his faith, was preaching one Sunday Morning at Hardoon Road Church in Shanghai. Watchman observed the congregation from his wooden seat at the side of the platform. As usual, he had prepared his message with extraordinary care for the specific needs of his listeners. Lately he was aware of how hard they were working at living the impossible Christian lifestyle, only to find themselves fighting spiritual dryness and discouragement.

He stood and walked to the corner of the lectern, leaning on it casually, looking from face to face among the crowd. He began his sermon.

"I will tell you a parable about a centipede I knew once," he announced brightly. His audience was already attentive. "One day, as my friend, the centipede, was about to go for a walk, he examined his legs to consider which one should move first. Should the left leg move first or the right one? How about the eighth leg or the tenth? The Centipede was a victim of self-paralysis, stuck there trying to decide which

leg to move first! The problem of the mind became a problem of practice."

As was his custom, Watchman paused and waited for the half finished parable truth to sink in.

"But if you don't know which leg to move first, how can you ever begin a journey?" asked Wu-chen Chang, three rows back on the right side.

"By giving no consideration to the problem in the first place," answered Watchman, seeing his opportunity to teach a great truth. "We all work too hard at being religious. God is much easier to live with than we are with ourselves. As Paul said to his friends in Ephesus, simply 'walk in His love.'"

"But what happened to the centipede?" came a question from his left. Watchman turned to engage the open expression of an eight-year-old girl named Mary Yu. Her winsome smile warmed his heart as he replied.

"Eventually, the sun came up," he said, his eyes shining with enthusiasm. "Without thinking, our little centipede friend ran out to see the sunrise without considering which leg to move first. He forgot about how to walk and simply walked. When the problem of the mind was gone, the problem of the practice also disappeared." Watchman stepped down from the platform and walked among his congregation, warming to the task.

"The truth is that the more you try to deal with inner dryness, depression, and flatness, the more they will overcome you. They become an issue only because we make them an issue. If you will forget them and let them go, they will disappear."

"But doesn't this 'forget them business' contradict what you've taught us before?" asked John Chang, his co-worker and friend, sitting on the front row. "Haven't you instructed us many times to fight against the devil?"

"No, dear friend," Watchman gently replied. "Resisting the devil is far different from trying to fight him on your own. You will lose the battle every time. The enemy can only be overcome by *the blood of the Lamb (Revelation 12:10)*. You resist him by hiding in Christ. Besides, resisting the devil is not the same thing as spiritual dryness. You conquer discouragement and the tyranny of impossible religious expectations by giving them no credibility. True faith is not about you trying; it's about you *dying*. It never was your battle. It's God's battle and He's already won it!"

Watchman then quoted The Book, *Philippians 1:21, "For me to live is Christ and to die is gain."* "You see it now, don't you? We labor all our lives to be Christ-like, only to find that such a goal was impossible from our first effort. We struggle to be more Christ-like and grow more discouraged daily when it doesn't happen. He simply wants us to live out His life within us. For me to live is Christ. It is Christ Himself living through us; speaking, witnessing, fathering, befriending, writing and singing: through us!"

Several in the congregation that day were released from the grind of working to earn God's favor and were set on the excellent path of learning to live in His grace.

Bob McLeod

As Dale lay motionless in his hospital bed paralyzed by self-consciousness, God had a Word for him. It's the same Word for you and me:

"My child, Jesus is the One Who created you, the One Who knows your every thought. He's with you now and He loves you with a passionate, unfailing love. He's not mad at you. He's not ashamed of you. He shed His precious blood that day at Calvary in order for you to be forgiven. He's here to help you. It's very important that you forgive everyone, including yourself! Jesus will help you. Receive His love and let Him remove your guilt, your regret and your shame. Your relationship with Him is all that matters."

We Dig Our Own Grave

26 Years old, he stares at the wall in the nursing home.
No one's home at all. The drugs took his mind. We pray not his soul.
Can he be saved? He dug his own grave.

We Dig Our Own Grave. We dig them deep.
We Dig Our Own Grave as Heaven weeps.
We must be so depraved. We just keep on Digging Our Own Grave.

Just look at that tree. You shall not die. Adam and Eve fell for the lie.
Now down through the ages their babies cry,
So betrayed. My God, they dug our own grave.

WWMD What Would Mohammed Do?

From the time that they're born we fill them with hate
Through the TV shows, videos, and the movies they rate.
Tune to violent cartoons and it's a fool who wonders why
There's murder in our schools.

He came for His own, yet He was despised.
They could not see He was God in disguise.
They nailed Him to a cross, He died but He came out of that grave,
Now He's alive and mighty to save those who:
Dig their own grave. We dug them deep.
We dug our own grave but Heaven had a promise to keep.
By His grace we are saved
No longer digging our own grave!

Bob McLeod

The Teddy Bear

I can see him, but only from a distance. I can hear the faint echo of his sobbing.

As I move closer, I begin to see the little boy more clearly. He's alone, abandoned, terribly frightened, trembling, and desperately clinging to his Teddy Bear.

He's obviously starving. His little belly is swollen, and gnats are swarming around his eye sockets.

As I continue to move closer, I can see his eyes—eyes filled with confusion, terror, suspicion and death. It's amazing how the eyes mirror the soul!

I feel so sorry for the child. I wish there were something I could do to help him.

Something or someone is drawing me closer to him. The closer I move, the faster I move. Then suddenly, with a *jerking flash*, I'm pulled inside the child, and I realize in an instant that *he is me!* I'm crying. I'm so thirsty! I'm cold! I'm afraid! Is anyone there? Somebody, please help me! My Teddy Bear is all I have. He has never hurt me! *I'll never let him go!"*

Then, out of nowhere, I hear a strange voice whisper my name. I'm afraid to look. I fall to the ground and curl my body around "Teddy."

Is the stranger going to take my teddy bear away? Is he going to hurt me or kill me? He whispers my name again. I begin to feel the warmth of his presence. He's coming closer and closer.

WWMD What Would Mohammed Do?

I look up and see Him. He's a large, powerful, kind-looking man. He's reaching down toward me.

"I love you," the man says. *"I'm here to help you. Don't be afraid. I won't hurt you. I've come to save you. Let me hold you."*

At first I don't trust him. I'm too afraid. But very gradually and cautiously I find myself beginning to surrender to the gentle stranger.

"Mister, if I come to you, do I have to leave my Teddy Bear?" I timidly ask.

The kind man doesn't say a word. *He simply stoops down and gently embraces me, Teddy Bear and all. I surrender.*

Suddenly, I'm on the outside again—an observer. The child has disappeared. As I look for him, I notice that I'm standing in front of a huge, luxurious, mansion. Its splendor is beyond description.

The big house is filled with light, life and bright music. I can hear children laughing and playing inside. The mansion is a place of joy, health and life.

Somehow I realize that one of the children inside the house is the same little boy who, just a few moments before, was outside clinging to his Teddy Bear and dying. And I know it's me! *I would recognize my laughter anywhere!*

Now what's that lying on the ground there in the *shadows?* I move closer to see. Why, it's a discarded, ragged Teddy Bear! It's the one the little boy was clinging to! But I can tell from the laughter coming from inside the house that he's okay without it! The little boy obviously doesn't need it anymore. He's forgotten all about the Teddy Bear that was so precious to him before.

The little boy is you. The little boy is me. *The little boy represents all of humanity.*

The Teddy Bear represents whatever we cling to in a futile effort to find life and survive. It can be *our religion, money, material possessions, drugs, or even another person.* It can be *power, prestige or a good reputation among men!*

Whatever we live for is our Teddy Bear. The Teddy Bear represents an idol. We cling to and are obsessed with "other gods" (Teddy Bears).

Deceived, we think that in them we can find life and fulfillment.

The kind gentleman is Almighty God. The mansion is referred to in the Book as:

Psalm 91:1
   "the Secret place of the Most High;
   "the Name of the Lord" in Proverbs 18:10,
   And "the Father's House" in John 14:2.

Notice what the kind gentleman did not say: He did not say, "get rid of that Teddy Bear, then you can enter my house and be blessed."

He did not say, "You ought to be ashamed of yourself. You're starving and dying, and it's all your fault. Get your act together! Then you can be one of mine."

He did not say, "Bow to the east five times a day, go to church, read your Holy Book, give 2 ½ or 10% of your Teddy

Bear to the Cosmic Vending Machine, quit eating for a month or gather a crowd."

The kind gentleman had mercy on the child. He understood that the child was helpless to save himself.

The child had legitimate needs. He needed food. He needed shelter He needed comfort. He needed love. He needed water. He was clinging to the only hope he thought he had— his Teddy Bear!

The child was trying to *meet his legitimate needs in an illegitimate way.* The Teddy Bear was dead, lifeless, and totally incapable of giving the little boy what he so desperately needed.

This, very simply, is the predicament and plight of humanity. We were born with the fallen nature of Adam. It's a nature addicted to idolatry, a nature that is totally alien and estranged from our Creator.

Two thousand years ago, God dressed up as a man, entered this planet and voluntarily became sin.

The Bible:
2 Corinthians 5:21
God made him who had no sin to be sin for us, so that in him we might become the righteousness of God.

This, in effect, was His way of embracing us, Teddy Bears (idols) and all. The only way He could approach us and reveal His unconditional love was by leaving the splendor of Heaven and coming into the Earth.

He knew He would be hated, rejected, and eventually killed by sin-sick people who were desperately and frantically clinging to their Teddy Bears (idols).

It was God's way of saying to us, "I love you. Let Me. I've prepared a place for you. I'm here to embrace you and to love you. The idols don't even matter. Let me love you, and you'll have the life you so desperately long for and need."

The Gospel is simply, "God loves you. Let Him." As you do, you will forget all about the Teddy Bears (idols). Idolatry (and the resulting sin) will no longer be an issue.

We don't need to grasp or cling to anything or anyone. Our life is in Christ. *He is the only One who can meet our legitimate needs in a legitimate way.*

God loves you, Teddy Bear and all. Simply receive His love and unconditional acceptance of you. As you do, *you will find life in abundance. He has promised and He can't lie!*

It's cold, lonely, and hostile in the front yard; but everything you need and could ever want is waiting for you in the kind Gentleman's House.

He doesn't condemn you. *He has a passion to embrace you, Teddy Bear and all!* Please let Him. You'll love it in the Father's House!

Let Me Love You
John 15:9

Working for Me is not the same as livin' for me.
I want you to see I long to live my life thru you.

WWMD What Would Mohammed Do?

I'm not really interested in your ministry.
I'm not really interested in how busy you can be.
My interest is in you.

Let Me Love You, Let Me Love You.
Let Me lift you high above your fear.
Let Me love you, Let Me Love You.
Let Me give you eyes to see
And ears to hear Me speak.
Let Me Love You.

Child, you've been striving for so long.
Fighting to find a way to feel like you belong.
But can't you see I love you just like you are.
I've already freely given you the very thing you've been grasping for.

Bob McLeod

Pathway to Intimacy

The Arabic word, Islam means *"a commitment to submit and surrender to God so that one could live in peace."* Peace *(salam)* is *achieved* according to Islamic scholars, through active obedience to the revealed commandments of God.

There is a very subtle yet profound and significant difference between surrender to a living God, as opposed to surrender to an interpretation of God's commandments. If surrender of self could be achieved, then it wouldn't be surrender. It would be self-effort. Obedience to commands follows surrender of self, not obedience in order to surrender.

God is indeed alive, and His heart is that we know and love Him. He mercifully and bountifully provides the way and the means for us to become intimate with Him. He desires for us to know Him personally.

Patti Brown was a beautiful marching ballerina. I was an ugly linebacker. *(My neck was larger than my head and my head was very large!)* Patti was prim, proper, pure, petite, feminine, gracious and graceful. I was agile, hostile, wild, crude, rude and temperamental (half temper, half mental!) She was the proverbial china shop; I was the proverbial bull; two absolutely opposite temperaments and personalities.

She was coming out of the Jacksonville State University cafeteria when I first saw her. My heart stopped. For the first time ever, I felt shy, insecure, and self-conscious. I wanted so much to know her but I knew I wasn't good enough for Patti Brown.

WWMD What Would Mohammed Do?

I remember being so disgusted with myself for not having lived a clean life. If only I hadn't been so crude; if only I had taken my education and future more seriously; *if only I were a better person, maybe then Patti Brown would be interested in me.*

"She won't give me the time of day," I thought. And even though I had no hope of her ever being interested in me, I still made sure I was outside the cafeteria each day when she was scheduled to appear. I tried so hard to keep my cool and not let anybody notice me noticing her. I had a major, big-time crush on the ballerina, Patti Brown.

I finally got up enough nerve one day to speak to her. I just happened (on purpose) to be walking in as she was walking out.

"Hello," I said.

She glanced at me, smiled that unforgettable, magic, grab-your-heart smile, and replied, "Hi."

I nearly flipped!

"I've got to meet her and get to know her!" I thought. "Maybe I could just be one of her friends. Maybe we could have lunch together."

"I know! I'll show up early tomorrow. Maybe I can sit at the same table with her. I mustn't appear to be too forward and eager though. That would ruin everything!"

Sure enough, the next day I skipped class and got there an hour early. After waiting impatiently, trying not to appear too conspicuous, I saw Patti Brown laughing and walking with some friends toward the cafeteria. I began to sort of slowly and nonchalantly strut and shuffle toward the chow line. Though my heart was racing, I had both hands down in my pockets, shoulders reared back, whistling a tune, as if I were the least concerned, got-it-all-together, coolest dude on campus!

I was able to sit next to Patti Brown that day and, over a period of time, I was comfortable enough to let my guard down and get real. Patti and I did become friends—best friends. *I'm still getting to know her and my love for her increases each day.* We've been married since June 14, 1969.

What a treasure she is! She's been a faithful wife, devoted mother, and a committed teacher to hundreds of children over these past three decades.

Looking back on our life together, we have cared for one another and each of our three children during health and sickness. We've taken in and cared for numbers of other people who had nowhere else to go. We grieved together as we buried both of our dads, many other close relatives and friends. We've known financial prosperity and near financial ruin.

There's been Cub Scout Den Meetings, little league games, dance recitals, Vacation Bible Schools, baptisms, camping trips, graduation ceremonies, Easter Egg hunts, Christmas trees, broken bones, dislocated limbs, all-night bedside vigils, and countless birthday celebrations.

We've cried together, laughed together, worried together and praised God together. *Each and every experience has made us more aware of our closeness to God and therefore, our closeness to each other.*

There have certainly been seasons of misunderstanding, miscommunication and disappointment over these years. We've both selfishly hurt each other's feelings too many times, but a simple and sincere, "I'm sorry" has always stilled the storm of surface emotion, and over and over again, *the healing balm of unfailing love has prevailed.*

Though our temperaments and personalities are still very different, we've enjoyed an overall unity, harmony and companionship that is the very essence of what a marriage is suppose to be. *I dearly love and remain faithful to my wife and I know, without a doubt, she loves and remains faithful to me.*

What is the purpose of marriage? Why does one human being get to know another and in particular, what does the marriage covenant mean?

Either there is a transcending and unending significance to our friendship and marriage, or else we're hopelessly headed for the most cruel and catastrophic collision there could ever be. One rapidly approaching day, (no matter how much Patti and I love each other, no matter how mutually dependent we may be), either she will bury me or I will bury her. We are destined to one day physically say, "goodbye." And that day may come suddenly and unexpectedly!

Parting of the Ways
Psalm 23:4

Bob McLeod

My way was letting go, then our way became holding on.
Girl, you know I hate to go and leave you here crying and all alone,
But there comes a time in every life declared Independence Day.
Sooner or later all Lovers have a Parting of The Ways.

The children we love so grow up overnight it seems
But loved ones come and they go,
Reminding us of what freedom really means.
I'm not complaining nor claiming life's all that cruel,
But sometimes it sure seems that way,
'Cause sooner or later all lovers have a Parting of The Ways.
Just keep on believing and lovin' and embracing Him,
Knowing we'll be together again one endless day.
This life is but a season
And you and me, we share the same rhyme and reason,
And an endless love Who shines and shows us the way.
So dry your eyes, you can smile and realize,
He'll never leave us,
He'll never forsake us,
Come what may.

When Jesus is your first love,
There'll soon be no more
Parting of the Ways.

Hope only comes as we discover the deeper wonder, eternal significance and mystery of shared love: **intimacy.**

The purpose of our becoming intimate with each other is in order that we might discover the pathway to intimacy with our Creator! Herein lies our hope and our purpose for being: the ultimate, intimate marriage union and love affair that never ends!

Ephesians 5:31,32
"For this cause shall a man leave his father and mother, and shall be joined unto his wife, and they two shall be one flesh. This is a great mystery: but I speak concerning Christ and the church."

The husband is to be a type and representation of the Lord Jesus Christ.

Ephesians 5:25
"Husbands, love your wives, even as Christ also loved the church, and gave himself for it.

The wife is to be a type and representation of the true church.

Ephesians 5:22-24
"Wives, submit yourselves unto your own husbands, as unto the Lord. For the husband is the head of the wife, even as Christ is the head of the church: and he is the Savior of the body. Therefore as the church is subject unto Christ, so

let the wives be to their own husbands in every thing." (Note: This is not submission to domination and control but rather, submission to love and care.)

Members of the true church are getting to know the Lord Jesus Christ in the same way that a wife and husband get to know each other. A man gives himself to his wife and to her alone. The woman gives herself to her husband and to him alone. This is what covenant is all about.

In the self-sacrificing and faithful love covenant, intimacy is nurtured and developed. *Love is the energy of that intimacy.* Two separate people literally become one.

Our Lord Jesus Christ's prevailing passion is relationship. He desires to be intimate with His people. *He wants you to know Him!* How is this accomplished?

The pathway to ever progressing, deeper intimacy is **_"trust and responding faithfulness."_** A healthy relationship typically begins on the surface level. When I first said, "hello" to Patti Brown, I was trusting her with a very surface part of me. Patti could have snubbed me, ignored me and hurt me, yet, she was faithful, considerate of my feelings, and when she returned my greeting with a simple "hi" and a smile, a relationship was born. As we have spent time together, our trust has deepened and our hearts have become more open to each other; *two people becoming one, growing in a wonderful relationship with each other through trust and responding faithfulness.*

It must be noted here that, when trust is betrayed, love is violated and intimacy is no longer there. *True love is unconditional, but trust must be earned.* Trust always leaves us vulnerable, and the depth of that trust determines the depth of our vulnerability. *The deeper the trust, the deeper the pain of being betrayed.*

Do you feel that the Lord Jesus Christ couldn't possibly have the time of day for you? Have you recognized that He is perfect and you're so imperfect? Do you have a personal sense of disgust and shame because, in the light of His perfection, you know you haven't lived right and you realize that you have no legitimate right to approach Him? Do you see how your unfaithfulness has so grieved and hurt Him as He's been quietly waiting for you?

Or perhaps you're so caught up in being the great pretender that you think other people are beneath you. Your identity may be in a "profit/loss statement," your reputation among men, or your knowledge of a holy book. *You might be concerning yourself with how impressive you think you are.* If this is the case, then you need to quit acting like you're the coolest dude on campus, stop your strutting and shuffling and get real. Look in the mirror and see what a self-centered, prideful and egotistical fool you are *without Christ.* You're a nobody. He's the King. Realize that there is no justifiable reason at all for Him to give you the time of day. No reason, that is, except His unfailing love for you.

If you haven't already, why not begin by trusting Him with at least a surface part of you? Look at Him hanging in writhing agony on that blood-soaked cross crying, *"Father forgive them, they know not what they do."*

153

Realize that He was crying out on your behalf! He gave His life in order that He might approach you and offer His hand and heart to you. Trust Him and receive His invitation of forgiveness and reconciliation. *He's offering you a marriage proposal.* No prenuptial agreement. His love is forever and without condition. And though you have been unfaithful, you will still find Him faithful to forgive you, and your relationship with Him will begin!

It mustn't stop there, however. As you learn to trust Him, your life will become a joy-filled journey of coming to know Him more and more intimately through every experience!

Do you need a Savior? *Trust Him. He will save you!* Do you have a daily need for power to overcome temptation and sin? *Trust Him. He will continually fill you with His All-Powerful Holy Spirit!* Do you need provision? *Trust Him. All of your needs are met according to His riches in glory!* Have you been betrayed by another? *Trust Him. He will bind up your broken heart and give you the ability to forgive!* Are you grieving over the physical loss of a dear loved one? *Trust Him. Jesus will fill the void and emptiness in your heart with none other than Himself!*

The following verse from the Book has been called the capsule verse of all Scripture, the one verse upon which all others hinge:

Proverbs 3:5,6
 "Trust in the Lord with all thine heart; and lean not unto thine own understanding. In all thy ways acknowledge him, and he shall direct thy paths."

The word *"acknowledge"* here is translated from the Greek word, "yada" which means, *"to know."* It's the same word used in

Hosea 2:20:
"I will even betroth (marry) *thee unto me in faithfulness: and thou shalt know* (yada) *the Lord.*

Jeremiah uses the same word when referring to the new covenant:

Jeremiah 31:34:
"And they shall teach no more every man his neighbor, and every man his brother, saying, Know (yada) *the Lord: for they shall all know* (yada) *me, from the least of them unto the greatest of them, saith the Lord; for I will forgive their iniquity, and I will remember their sin no more.* Hallelujah!

When you trust in the Lord with **all** of your heart, not leaning on your own understanding, you will always find Him faithful. *Your confidence in Him will grow and your trust will naturally deepen.* You're now on the pathway to ever progressing, deeper intimacy with Him!

The troubles, trials, suffering, strain and pain of this life is all orchestrated by God to reveal to each of us, in a very personal way, how helpless we are. *The intent of revealed helplessness is to lead us to a deeper trust in Him.*

Bob McLeod

The Song of Songs is an often-overlooked part of the Book. It was written by Solomon and is a beautiful story about an intimate love affair between a Shulamite maiden and her handsome lover. Many Christians are embarrassed to study this book, but it's very important to see what God is showing us here.

Allegorically, it pictures Israel as God's betrothed bride and *the church as the bride of Christ.* As human life finds its highest fulfillment in the love of a man and woman, so spiritual life finds its highest fulfillment in the love of God for his people; and *Christ for His church.*

Solomon also wrote Ecclesiastes, the book, which precedes *the Song of Songs. The sequence of these two books is significant.* Solomon had it all, tried it all and concluded that everything under the sun is vanity! He then moves into the Song of Songs and we see where true fulfillment and happiness are found: not under the Sun*, but in an intimate love affair with the Son!*

In *Song of Songs 1:2* we read the passionate cry of the Shulamite maiden, *"Let Him kiss me with the kisses of His mouth—for your love is better than wine!"* We only have one mouth; therefore a kiss on the mouth is one-on-one! *Only you, only Him.*

Have you trusted Him? If so, you are finding Him forever and always faithful! But don't ever forget, you have a part in this relationship. He's faithful to you. *Are you faithful to Him?*

"Lord, what are You trusting me to do? Give 2 1/2 or 10% of my money? Pray five times a day? Attend church or mosque? Quit eating for a month? Study my holy book? Attend Hajj or a Billy Graham Crusade?"

He softly and patiently replies, *"No. None of those things."*

"Then, what is it? Have my daily devotion, quiet time, witness to people? Preach the Gospel? Help the poor? Raise money? What are you trusting me to do? I want to get on with it! I'm committed Lord!"

"Child, you can never do right to be right."

"Then, what are you trusting me to do, Lord?"
Be quiet, still and listen. He's waiting to speak to you.
"Child, I'm simply trusting you to trust Me."

"Do right to be right" is self-justification and legalism. Legalism is deadly because it's an insult and an affront to God's offer of intimacy. He demonstrated His love for us at Calvary that dark day two thousand years ago. When we try to earn that which He freely offers, we are rejecting Him!

Trust in God
Proverbs 3:5,6

What do you do when the money's all gone? Trust in God.
What do you do when you feel so alone? Trust in God.
What do you do when you're so broken-hearted?
What do you do when the Red Sea's not parted?

Bob McLeod

What do you do when you don't know which way to turn?
That's when you learn to Trust in God.

What do you do when your friends all forsake you?
Trust in God.
What do you do when sin overtakes you? Trust in God.
What do you do when your world falls around you?
What do you do when sorrow surrounds you?
What do you do when you don't know which way to turn?
That's when you learn to Trust in God.

I know I ought to
But I don't always do what I ought to do.
So please don't scold me
Just simply show me how to
Trust in God.

What do you do when there are no heartbeats left?
What do you do as you breathe your last breath?

WWMD What Would Mohammed Do?

The Well

If the sun's rays could reach the pavement, eggs would fry there. Dry scorching heat. No breeze. People gasping. Packed like sardines. Suffering and death. Can't move. Dead bodies upright. No place to fall. Stench. Dehydration. Thirst. Torture. Death. Hell on earth.

In the distance I can see a well. People are crowding all around it. Some of them are obviously leaders. With a holy book in one hand and a bucket in the other, they drop their buckets into the well, bringing them back up full of water. They pass it out into the crowd for the people to drink. It's life-giving water. People are fighting over it.

No, wait a minute! It should be giving life but it's not! *Those who drink from the buckets are dying faster than those who have nothing to drink.*

I don't understand. I've got to get to that well. With the last ounce of energy that's left within me, I cry out to the Heavens.

"Help! I must get free from these people! I must get to that well! Someone, anyone, please free me from these people!"

Then, from out of what I thought was nowhere, comes a sword, a two-edged sword. It cuts me free from the others. It severs a cord that I didn't even realize was there, a cord that had me bound to the others in the crowd, a three-strand cord.

Instantly, I'm at the well. I look down inside. Wow! I've never seen anything like it, pure, crystal clear, sparkling, life-giving water. There's hope!

"Someone give me a drink!" No wait a minute! Those who drink die faster. I don't understand.

Then I remember the One with the sword, the One from the place I thought was nowhere.

He heard my cry before. Maybe He'll hear me now. "Sir, why? Why does life-giving water kill?"

Then, in a still, small voice more clear than any human voice, and in a language more understandable than any human tongue, I hear Him in my mind.

"The buckets are man-made, not God-made. The people are drinking contaminated water. Whenever a fleshly human hand touches my life giving-water, it becomes defiled. Death replaces life."

"My God, what can I do? People are dying of thirst and here before me is the life-giving water that will save them. I dare not touch it! But what can I do? I feel so helpless! What can I do?"

He speaks again. The simplicity and quietness of His Words are almost deafening:

"Fall in the well and become the water." His voice echoes again and again. *"Fall in the well and become the water. Fall in the well and become the water. Fall in the well..."*

I'm willing. Life can be found nowhere else. I let go. I surrender all that I have and all that I am. I fall. The water begins to fill me. Like intense, but gentle, pulsating waves of liquid love, the water begins to swirl around me, and even through me!

Thank God! Living Water! I'm being filled! I'm being strengthened! I'm being healed. Then, I feel my body being lifted. My heart remains in the well, but somehow my physical body returns to the crowd of people. I'm no longer attached to them, but I'm still with them.

I find myself giving instead of taking. I find myself being used rather than using others. I find myself forgiving those who have wronged me.

I no longer have any hidden agenda. *I love people!* I love them without expectation! I love them without condition! I love them no matter what they do. We are all on the same level. None rich. None poor. None strong. None weak. None black. None white. None male. None female. All, like myself, are in constant need of the living water.

Some receive me. Some reject me. Some despise me. Some respect me. Others ignore me. It no longer matters. They don't have to love me, for me to love them. I love them with living water.

One day very soon, I'll leave the crowd of people and this troubled place. My time of giving and serving will be over. I'll return to the well, never to be seen here again. The well keeps calling me. The well is my home. He and I have become one. *I am the water.*

John 7:38
"Whoever believes in me, as the Scripture has said, streams of living water will flow from within him."

Bob McLeod

Song of Solomon 4:15

"You are a garden fountain, a well of flowing water streaming down from Lebanon."

Matthew 10:39

"Whoever finds his life will lose it, and whoever loses his life for my sake will find it."

John 17:20-23

"My prayer is not for them alone. I pray also for those who will believe in me through their message, that all of them may be one, Father, just as you are in me and I am in you. May they also be in us, so that the world may believe that you have sent me. I have given them the glory that you gave me, that they may be one as we are one: I in them and you in me. May they be brought to complete unity to let the world know that you sent me and have loved them, even as you have loved me."

Proverbs 5:15

"Drink water from your own cistern, running water from your own well."

Jeremiah 23:15-16

"Therefore, this is what the Lord Almighty says concerning the prophets: 'I will make them eat bitter food and drink poisoned water, because from the prophets of Jerusalem ungodliness has spread throughout the land.' This is what the Lord Almighty says: 'Do not listen to what the prophets are prophesying to you; they fill you with false hopes. They speak visions from their own minds, not from the mouth of the Lord.'"

1 Corinthians. 6:17
"But he who unites himself with the Lord is one with him in spirit."

Galatians 3:28
"There is neither Jew nor Greek, slave nor free, male nor female, for you are all one in Christ Jesus."

Hebrews 4:12
"For the word of God is living and active. Sharper than any double-edged sword, it penetrates even to dividing soul and spirit, joints and marrow; it judges the thoughts and attitudes of the heart."

1 John 2:16
"For everything in the world—1) the cravings of sinful man, 2) the lust of his eyes and 3) the boasting of what he has and does—comes not from the Father but from the world."

Amen. Peace be within you.

Bob McLeod

Have You Seen Jesus?
Galatians 3:28

*They called Jesse a no count, colored man.
He lived in a shack on the outskirts of town.
The City Council was considering tearing
That embarrassing eyesore down.*

*One morning during rush hour, you know how children are,
A little girl got away from her mommy,
Ran out in front of a speeding car.
Jesse got there just in time to push the child out of harm's way.
That so-called, no count, colored man gave his life
Saving the mayor's daughter that day.
Have you seen Jesus? He's a black man.*

*Jesus is a black man and as a white man he has been seen.
Jesus is black; Jesus is white and everything in between.
Have you seen Jesus? He's a black man.*

*Bowie was white and 17. He joined the Army Corps.
Found himself fighting in Viet Nam in that unholy war.
Surrounded by the enemy, His black friend was saved
When Bowie threw himself on an exploding hand grenade.
Have you seen Jesus? He's a white man.*

That was Him under a veil crying in Afghanistan.

WWMD What Would Mohammed Do?

He's a father, He's a mother, He's a child, He's a woman and a man.

You can find Him in a back street bar or sometimes under a steeple

He's anywhere you are, living and loving all kinds of people.
Have You Seen Jesus?

Bob McLeod

WWMD What Would Mohammed Do?

Epilogue

The Only Superpower
Isaiah 40:15

In a world filled with trouble; in an age of uncertainty,
Fear demands make friends with evil,
Give your blessings to the thieves.
Even though the sea is raging, some say don't dare rock the boat.
Negotiate with murderers or else there's just no hope.
So they bow every hour before their so-called superpowers,
At the feet of their ivory towers, while the enemy devours
Innocent men, innocent women, and precious babies.

Spread the Word throughout the world
Of the Glorious Light that we see.
There's just one Almighty King bringing enemies under His feet.
Those who deny Him will perish. Those who love Him will be fed.
And His judgment will be passed
For every drop of blood that's been shed
By innocent men, innocent women, and precious babies.

The only Superpower is Jesus Christ.
The only Superpower is Jesus Christ.

Bob McLeod

We will not fear the evil one, for darkness must yield to the Light!
There's only one Superpower, Jesus Christ.

Politicians just come and they go.
The wisdom of man is but a foolish dream.
The only hope is a Holy Ghost revival like the world ain't never seen!
It's time to take up the shield of faith, draw out your two edged sword,
Adorn the breastplate of righteousness
And pray for the day of the Lord!

About the Author

Bob McLeod is a Preacher. His Congregation is the world. His guitar is his pulpit. His songs are his sermons.

Bob and his wife, Patti make their home in the Williams Community near Jacksonville, Alabama, USA.

WWW.BROKENSTONE.ORG

Printed in the United States
18888LVS00013B/100